POETRY RIVALS 2012

THE PROBING PEN

Edited by Donna Samworth

First published in Great Britain in 2012 by:
Forward Poetry
Remus House
Coltsfoot Drive
Peterborough
PE2 9BF
Telephone: 01733 890099
Website: www.forwardpoetry.co.uk

FOREWORD

In 2009, Poetry Rivals was launched. It was one of the biggest and most prestigious competitions ever held by Forward Poetry. Due to the popularity and success of this talent contest like no other, we have taken Poetry Rivals into 2012, where it has proven to be even bigger and better than previous years.

Poets of all ages and from all corners of the globe were invited to write a poem that showed true creative talent - a poem that would stand out from the rest.

We are proud to present the resulting anthology, an inspiring collection of verse carefully selected by our team of editors. Reflecting the vibrancy of the modern poetic world, it is brimming with imagination and diversity.

As well as encouraging creative expression, Poetry Rivals has also given writers a vital opportunity to showcase their work to the public, thus providing it with the wider audience it so richly deserves.

CONTENTS

THE POEMS

STRONG

Someone out there make me strong
I have been weak for so long
Make me feel that I belong
Make me see right from wrong

At great length
Someone give me strength

Do not let me go away
With you I want to stay
Do not ever let me go astray
Do not let me find somewhere new to play
Give me blue skies and take away the clouds so grey
I want to be with you each and every day
Be with me always, come what may

Teach me in life what is right
Help me in times of plight
Make each day ever so bright
Take away the fear, take away the fright
Help me see the light

Help me live a life so straight
Be my friend, be my soulmate
Because I love you, I think you are great
Be with me and do not let me get in a sad state
You are someone I could never hate
You never get upset with me, you never get irate

Always be with me
Unchain me and set me free
That is what I want, that is my plea
Give me a love that knows no degree

Be with me when I call
Do not let me slip, do not let me fall
All I want is you, that is all

With you I feel in paradise
With you I feel ever so nice.

Wally

THE APPIAN WAY

The Appian Way winds
Amid fields of malachite
And white marble stems
And beautiful grave monuments
Buried alive amid
Time and green
The winding stems of shrubbery
And joyous twittering of birds.
The Appian Way winds
Beneath the honeycomb
Of a thousand empty –
Graves.
(Dust long ago carried off by tourists,
As a memento of sunny summer
And the sweat of love;
They make it
In cars what stand by the roadside)
The Appian Way winds
Above the black pores
Of catacombs,
Awaiting resurrection
(As the great pyramids
Of Giza also await it.
They stand,
Grinning with their centuries,
Their ribbed facets.
Among the yellow
Waving sands,
Which move into the horizon
Of a pure clear sky).
Fish, scratched onto the walls:
They're distinguishable with difficulty
And the guide helpfully points a flashlight.
It is wise and prudent
To invest capital in immortality –
It's all cheap and simple:
You have to live in catacombs
And believe
Though afterwards the death
Is often not a martyr's.
A plain old death.
The usual.
(Four hundred billion deaths
Have already occurred on the planet.

Often just
Standard deaths,
Just like yours and mine:
An ordinary agony and death rattle.)
This wise democracy of nature:
It doesn't tolerate egocentrics
Who wish to live forever.
Four hundred billion
That's almost twice as many
As the number of suns in our galaxy:
A provincial whitish spot
Amid
A numberless number of others
The Appian Way winds
And seems endless
(That's just an illusion and a lie,
For everything in this world has an end.)
The suns sets
And evening arrives
(This is inevitable
And therefore necessary
It's calm in relation
To evening and the night
That follows after.)
But my blood
Freezes
(Blood may freeze
Even in Italy
Especially in spring
And I recommend that everyone
Who plans to go to Italy in spring
Bring a store of warm clothes.)
And I turn around
And go to Rome.
Whither goest thou?
I go to Rome,
Because I have
No other way out.
If you
Know a way out,
Then write a letter.
Or better yet
Beat it out
On the wall of the temple of Karnak,
Where the great Ramses
Sprinkles the tiny figures

Of the Hetts with arrows
And crushes them
With his chariot wheels
He goes so high
That I can barely
Distinguish
His godly features
On the rays of the spotlight
On the background of black night sky
Sprinkled with chilly
Galactic crystals.

Dmitry Shlapentokh

30 SECONDS TO END THE 18 MONTHS

I was deceptive, too deceptive.
I didn't even see it after it had been done,
I became its detective.
I had the evidence,
I prosecuted and the verdict of today was the elective.
We had done it, something we should have done a long time ago?
It's a shame it took its time to show,
Now and back in our time in the low.

Here I saw the logic and it was undeniable,
Well constructed, fitted and flyable.
It would help all in the picture,
Giving them the correct colours for the context;
To make it classifiable.
It seems pictures of this sort are not meant to be correct and at the most common, downright
unreliable.

So I thought I'd move and maybe take a few good leaps,
Find something again, maybe this time for keeps.
But it seems the past is the past, and you can't keep jumping back into it,
Giving everyone you knew the creeps.
So I've accidently plunged myself into the deeps,
The stars and night's air will yet again be that friend;
Till I see and ascend to the state where I can unbend.

Jack Shimmin

RALLY

To me brave boys, to me now!
Come rally to the flag.
Prepare to meet our enemy
Let not your spirits sag.

Reform your ranks around me
Take heart and stand with pride.
Draw forth your swords with honour,
Let's break this heathen tide!

Let not their numbers daunt you
Stand firm against the flood.
Make every forward step they take
Be paid for with their blood.

They shall not take our homelands
Our bones are of this Earth
A thousand years we've dwelt here
This land is ours by birth!

The battle will soon be upon us,
Our mettle must not sway.
Give our sons a tale to tell their sons
Let's make history this day!

Mick Clark

JEAN

Jean we know is sixty-five
Thus autumn in her breast must live,
While unlocked through a sweet smile,
Summer in her face is seen and her face is seventeen,
Jean's heart dreams wistful fancies,
For her vernal days,
Yet her allure still invites our gallantry,
Yes Jean we know is sixty-five,
And in her face a question did arise,
Which were more beautiful, her lips or eyes?
I think her eyes still send forth those pointed darts,
That can pierce the hardest adamantine heart,
Yet from her lips proceed those sweet blisses
Which I still reap by kind words and sweet kisses.

Tony Beeby

WINSTON

Such a sweet boy am I,
An apricot point Siamese,
With a striped tail that curls over.
With an adorable face,
You'll notice my blue eyes
Grow larger when I see food
Or Mummy.
I love to cuddle
Up on a lap.
I'm a cheeky chap really
When you get to know me.
And when I the sleep
I make the cutest
Faces.
Watch me as I run
Quickly
To greet my human
Family.
Oh
Don't you think I'm
Just a sweetheart?

Jessica Stephanie Powell

FLAMES ON THE FROST

Misted windows gasp and shiver
As they wake to the winter-feathered fishbone sky,
Bread and butter clouds, narrow snowline river,
An iron wind that bites hard and dry.

A shy, honeyed, rosy globe tests the icy morning
But searching finds no scattered dew,
Only stubborn solid pools and frosty patterns forming.
Drawing back her stretching fingers
Now growing numb, pale and stiff; she no longer lingers.

Etched flowing ferns and snowflakes dance,
Cut deep into the ice they catch her sparkling glance.
Slowly there drives a fierce desire
To prove her strength, cast her flames, her greatest chance
To fill this frosted world with fire.

Alison Hodge

THE MAGICAL MONTH

The month of May is magical
When all at once it seems
The natural world has come alive
A fragrant world of dreams
The blossom's all so beautiful
So artfully displayed
We wonder how they hid themselves
Before the new parade.

Here surely is the dawn of hope
When from the winter's chill
Such stunning beauty can emerge
From life no longer still.
So let's rejoice and celebrate
And take pleasure in its reign
For soon the summer fruits will come
And the cycle starts again.

Frank Flower

HIGH AND LOW

High aloft, adorned, to sit in metal tube
With wings of fuel and fire.
Far below, aged watch and muse.
A pension springs from such desire.

Up, yet further up, higher, higher to
Blue worlds of silence. And to wallow
Among island clouds, into that unchartered abyss
Where no birdsong could follow.

Here was no shadow before Man came,
Flitting fast across cloud below.
He rides with hope, there is no blame
For any stain upon the snow.

Each one leaving behind the echo
Of their flight, the carriages of kings
Rich and noble, marking the restless sky.
An unending river of wings.

Anne Palmer

HOLIDAY MADNESS

Breakfast on the veranda
Lunch overlooking the sea
Our tea we eat outside
Which we eat up happily

The sun is out, the sky is cloudless
The sea an inviting warm
Kids with nets go crab hunting
And sandcastles they do form

It's time to relax and chill out
A great way in which to unwind
The sun to tan your body
The fresh air to clear your mind

With family all around us
It's the beach that we do go
With laughs and giggles a-plenty
It's the water that we do throw

The children playing happily
Buckets and spades are fun
Their enjoyment is enormous
As they play out in the sun

The adults built the biggest castles
And pretend that they are three
And join in the kids with silliness
And splash around in the sea.

Carena Mills

FEUD

A lifetime of regret results from spite –
For words, once uttered, cannot be withdrawn.
Their poison seeps into the very soul
Of those alive (and even those unborn).

The time to put things right has slipped away –
As pride withholds the move to make amends.
Now silence reigns and hatred comes to stay,
Instead of warmth between two loving friends.

The years go by, while others join the fray –
And battle lines have now become entrenched.
The story, handed down, infects them all,
Their eyes stay closed and hands meet fists still clenched.

Ellen Green Ashley

A BALD BIRD

Who put that feather on the floor?
You naughty bird
I've told you before
Desist from plucking
You will feel the cold
Shivering featherless
Nothing with which to enfold
Your wingless body
Suppose you need to fly?
Flapping bare arms
You could only try
With little avail
I fear. Cease to pluck
Keep your feathers
As any other duck.

Betty Gilman

A GHOST OF A SMILE

I always hated that supercilious smile dear – the one you wore to put me down
Never a tender word dear – well not when I was around
One kind word wouldn't have gone amiss.
How could love be so cruel?
Hoping, waiting, for some small sign – that you cared – just a little
Six months to live they told me
How your face lit up with hope –
But not for me
'I'll come back to haunt you,' I said
You just smiled – that smile
But now the mighty has fallen dear –
A big strong man like you,
You lie here in your bed of steel –
Strange faces surrounding you
Yes, I've come back to haunt you dear –
With a malevolent stare and spitting tongue –
A hell on Earth where you belong.
It's time to face up to your demons dear,
I'll care for you whilst you sleep –
Place icy fingers on your fevered brow and spoil the fog of sleep.
I see that you are fading fast dear –
But stay a while with me.
I'll invade your dreams like you did mine –
Haunt you for the rest of time.
And if, in your restless sleep,
There's no respite for you,
Don't worry dear, open your eyes, open them and see – see me – and I'll smile – this smile.

Patricia Pulman

THE FAMILY HAVE BEEN INFORMED

Abruptly hurled together through death's dark door,
Unexpected visitors, untimely, unannounced,
Drawn with evil intent into a place of death
A place known to the enemy,
But not to them –

Explosives roar,
Debris spits against the sheer blue sky,
Blood stains the burning sand,
An obscene silence stops the clock's hand
They are no more –

Souls soar, slipping silently away.
Gently travelling towards the light,
Travelling towards their peace.
Blessed with courage, young brothers in arms.
In a breath have lost their fight,
Place a marker where they lay.

Full lives, yet all so brief,
Friends and loved ones will not touch them again,
They will also be broken, in their maze of grief,
There will be few words to describe the overwhelming pain,
In time's fullness treasured memories
Will give strength, and hope will return again.
Hearts may heal, but the wars will never be gone.

Gail Cureton

THE BROKEN ROSE!

Through the Safire rose blazed radiant pearls
All glistening in moonlight at the quench for lover's thirst,
It was like a desert sand where one craves for rain
It was like the meadows where a lonely man seeks a companion.
However this was about a young girl
She looked through mesmerised eyes
All passionate about the future and its lies.
Through the Safire rose showed broken pearls
All scattered on the floor, wet like tears
The heart was oozing, dripping in blood
The heart was a boat
Inside it, water did flood.
However this water was eternal love.
Overflowing like a fountain
It stopped and came to a shore
Lovers' love was finally off-board
The dejected eyes finally lost their smile
The eyes were burning like fire coal
The pain was piercing deep inside the soul.
Like fire burning on a desert night,
The thorn that hurt made her cry.
Weeping by the fire on a cold winter's night
The memories continued to agonise.
Through the Safire rose shone injured petals
Leaving a scar on the broken heart
Feelings of despair mesmerised her glare.
Gazing through gloomy eyes
The love she craved was no longer alive
Through the Safire rose was shown a broken rose
Petals all over the floor, in the scorching cold
Through the Safire rose was a wounded heart
Covered in tears, and lost in hurt.

Afsha Bi Farook

I AM LEOPARD

I am the one that walks alone, a death
In shadow. I am hunter. Predator in
velvet, undulating, smooth, fluid of
shape, one who melts away into the
black of Earth, the starless vault of sky.

I am a keen blade, fierce, all angles
hard as winter under snow. Blood
of ink runs in my veins. I am the cloak
invisible, listening for the heartbeat
and the breath. I sense. I wait.

I am the criminal who leaves no trace
the hairs that rise upon your neck
that sudden chill. I am ghost, floating
through the haunted air and touched by
moonlight. I am sorcerer, bewitching.

I am undercover silence. Fatal beauty,
lethal grace. Nature holds her breath as
I pass through her jungle night with eyes
of liquid fire. A searing heat across the
chocolate dark like ripe fruit, blazing.

Nicola Wood

SPARE TYRE

I want to do something naughty
I want to do something rude
I'll take off all my clothes
And sit here in the nude
I'll take off all my clothes
And sit here in the chair
I've got nothing to admire
Now I'm in my sixties
Wow look at that spare tyre.

Terry Knight

INSPIRED

I love to write prose,
And sometimes my poetry flows,
But there are times,
When I run out of rhymes,
Every morsel of my mind goes blank,
Empty is my think-tank,
Then something happens happy or sad,
And opens up my writing pad,
And here flows my poetry prose,
I write about my highs and lows,
It helps me through when I am down,
Helps me smile when I have to frown,
It dries away the tears,
Like when my cat died after 20 years,
And when I hear sad news of people I know,
And that they're dying, with not long to go,
Poetry helps me through my toils,
Especially when there come the spoils,
And life gets a little hard,
So when I'm feeling a little mard,
I pick up my pad and pen,
And write a poem there and then!

Theresa Hartley-Mace

SKYLARK

Bells ring quiet across the plain,
The skylark needs to sing again.
Stillness moves across her face,
A secret smile, the coolest embrace.
Such beauty rests behind life's veil,
Strength beyond the darkest pale.
Aching heart bleeds broken promise,
Missing finds its final solace.
I stand alone, daffodils weep
Fly skylark, let serenity sleep . . .

Bev Hickey

BIRDS

The Lord God made exquisite birds
That soar in flight on outstretched wings.
Their beauty far exceeds all words.
Unique soliloquies each sings.

Some birds have feathers drab and dull,
As camouflage from preying eyes,
While others are most colourful,
Which can their safety jeopardize.

The raven's black and augurs doom.
The gentle dove's a sign of peace.
The cock'rel, flaunting scarlet plume,
Announces when night's shadows cease.

Small sparrows; robins; wrens, and tits
Frequent our gardens day by day.
Among the reeds the warbler flits,
And seagulls brave the ocean spray.

Proud peacocks' clarion-calls are shrill.
Melodious is the speckled thrush.
On hov'ring wing, sweet skylarks trill,
And night-owls hoot in twilight hush.

Great mighty eagles circle high
Above the tow'ring mountain peaks.
Large flocks of geese traverse the sky
In ever-changing patterned streaks.

Oh! Had I wings, I'd flutter too.
O'er chimney tops and trees I'd rise,
While marv'lling at th'expanding view
Which greeted and beguiled my eyes.

Yet with the birds my heart ascends,
Transported from this earthly sphere,
To Heaven's vaults where bliss transcends,
And Paradise feels very near.

Eileen Nancy Blackmore

THE WARRIOR'S PRAYER

We left behind the sun
When our journey begun,
The Messenger and the Beauty,
Were left,
And Earth,
The place of our birth,
Passed Mars on our duty,
And the asteroid bereft,
The king of the gods,
And his father at all odds,
Uranus,
The wind at our backs,
Passed the mighty Neptune,
To seek our fortune,
And Pluto without a fuss,
With courage none of us lacks,
Heading for Acamar and Bellatrix,
Bright stars upon we fix,
Vega and Markab,
Deneb and Gemma,
Going for Australis,
In the deep blackness,
With all that we have,
Into the great beyond with honour.

Jonathan Luke Simms

SAID THE FLOWER

'Not for me,' said the flower,
'Is the bridal bouquet.
Give me not to a lover
On Valentine's Day.
Do not arrange me
To enhance an altar,
Nor buy me for wives
When marriages falter.
But take me now and throw me down
In the path if a soldier, carried home
Through the streets of a Wiltshire town.'

Anne Kinsey

16

TRAVELLING

(Any similarity to Auden's 'Night Mail' and to Tennyson's 'Lady of Shalott' is intentional)

On either side the river lie
a rail track and a motorway
that carry people back and forth
twixt Birmingham and Ampleforth.
In one direction thousands go
to Newcastle and Edinboro'
in comfortable seats of plush,
while others bear commuter rush
to office block and shop and bank,
with little time to stop and thank
their great Creator up above,
who offers life, protection, love.
Through fields of yellow oilseed rape
they travel on, nor heed to gape
at all the places speeding by:
The evidence of battle cry,
the castles, windmills, squat church towers,
brick cottages and orchard bowers,
where second-homers spend weekends
with grans and mums and kids and friends.
No more the steam train hoots aloud
to scare away the standing crowd
of cattle, black and white and brown,
but two-tone diesel horn, up – down
disturbs them little as they munch
on last year's hay, a welcome lunch.
Through darkish tunnels, over bridges,
and by the sides of mountain ridges,
they hurtle by, ears full of noise
of mobile phones and other toys.
White criss-crossed vapour trails belie
thousands of travellers in the sky
in silvery tubes of steel so strong,
piloted through the clouds along.
Commuters block the motorway lane,
and laden lorries, some from Spain,
creep onwards, onwards, through the night,
towards the service station's light.
Oh lucky me, to sit in peace,
and take retirement's rest and ease!

Joan Carter

PRAYER

No longer do we recall the Christian saints
When every Sunday some national sport is played
And churches are no longer full of worshippers
When crowds are watching cricket, tennis or football

The churches dwell frequently on sin and love
Whilst crowds at sport shout and cheer their side
Wearing their team's shirt they are obsessed by stars
Who now replace the saints we once admired

In the past on Sundays men wore their smartest suit
And seldom were allowed to play games or even cards
Now with alcohol support they scream and shout
And use of language never heard in church

Few worship now or talk to Christ
Where is the love of Christ that was so strong?
As now it is the green grass and not the altar
Where crowds instead of prayer, all shout to win.

But then there is still the power of prayer
By many with their Christian faith
Can influence our minds and hearts
And help us maintain our Christian faith.

John Veitch

TAKE MY HAND

Take my hand, I know the way,
Kneel down, and let us pray,
To the Lord, our God above
To send His blessing and His love,
To make this world a better place,
To help us with the trials we face,
Forgive us for our great mistakes,
Show mercy, please, for all our sakes,
So take my hand, dear Lord I pray,
And lead us to a better way.

Annie McKimmie

A TRUE FRIEND

A true friend is very hard to find.
One who touches your heart.
Someone who is understanding and kind,
With whom you never want to part.
A true friend lifts you up high
When your world is blue.
Is there when others pass you by,
Takes care and comforts you.
A true friend is one who knows your faults,
But loves you just the same.
Listens to your highs and lows.
But always plays the game!
Yes a true friend is always there
To share life's rugged way.
A shining gem beyond compare,
To treasure every day.

Josie Rawson

THE DAY

Sun shining
Clouds white,
Day bright and fresh. A new day dawns.
People walking, strolling down the path
Over to the woods,
Sea crashing in the distance,
Seagulls whirling in and out,
Out to sea and back in land.
People walking from the prom, on towards the beach.
Enjoying the day with chips and ice cream.
Sun shining bright,
Clouds white and grey,
Day bright and fresh,
What a lovely day.

A Mitchell

MY EXPERIENCE

With my case tightly packed
One onboard bag
We travelled to the airport
At the last moment my daughter gave me
A present for her brother
I didn't give it a second glance
I just thrust it into my bag
We made our way slowly down to check-in
Then onto security gate
When much to my surprise
I was taken to one side
And ordered to open my bag
I tried to explain my fingers were stiff
And I might need a helping hand
He looked at me and sternly said
'Please, Madam, open your bag'
He waited and waited . . .
After he had confiscated the present
With a slight grin
He explained it wasn't the fact it was Marmite
Just the volume of liquid inside
And if I wished pay tax for it
When we arrive back to UK
Needless to say, in spite of the loss
And my stupidity
I really appreciate our security
But will be more vigilant next time.

Christina Batley

BUS DRIVERS AND INSPECTORS

I have seen them, their coats flapping,
In draggled trousers;
Grime on a lady bus driver's face,
Like crows,
Tattered and squawking,
Or talking,
Steering into the wind,
Waiting there,
Littering the streets with their carcasses,
In higgledy-piggledy fashion;
Some talking together,
Some abandoned,
Buttoned up,
Utilitarian-looking,
And at last the bus arrives,
All disappear,
Climbing on-board,
Taking their dark frames with them.

Judith Fleetwood-Walker

LIFE'S BRIEF SPAN

I mourn each year that passes
As if it were a friend
For every year that passes
Brings me closer to my end

The years go by so swiftly
Each one following another
I have lost many dear to me
My parents, husband, brother

Yet we were all given
The power to remember
That we might have roses
In our December

And I have so many memories
To warm me and to cheer
Now the December of my life
Is almost here.

Shirley Brooks

LEAVING THE CITY

Flickers of light play on my speckled window
And I no longer want to meet the day,
My life pauses at amber lights
Before the city's get up and go.
Look at all those people so busy
Rushing to and coming from,
That they are going nowhere in-between.
All those businessmen with brollies
And zebra'd pinstriped suits,
Flashing by like a monochrome TV picture
Out of focus and will it
Rain in the world markets today?
Secretaries with keyboard pinched noses,
Click-clacking with typewriter high heel shoes
At sixty-one the minute.
Factory workers who wear their greasy overalls
As if of badges of office,
Whilst pretty girls look wistfully at the day
And not where they are going.

A mother scolds an erring child,
Beats it black and blue.
She needn't have taken the trouble
That's just what the world will do.
An angry young man
Who set out to change the world
Has just lost his place
In the long dole queue.
A puff of petrol fumes along the way
A red flash, a green flash
And nicotine-yellow too.
Smells of Costa Rica coffee
Along with stale British railway's brew.

Squeaky youngsters off to Woolies
When they should be sat in school,
Studying fast the machines
Many hammer-headed ways.
Lower down upon the church stone steps
A hungry tramp stirs
Casting off yesterday's papers,
Which read the same for every day.
The church will be open this Sunday.

And the praises will ring quite high

They will all be a lot nearer to Heaven
Than that old tramp or I.
A hustle here, a bustle there,
Some get to sit on government soft seats
Whilst others sleep on hard park benches.
A lean old seadog from old Tiger Bay
Stops at the crossing to rekindle
A battered pipe, he turns his craggy face
To leeward of a past trade wind.
And I wonder if he wonders
What's it all about?

There is my sister's house down that street,
She'll be at the window,
Looking out as she always does,
The window with the thick gloss ledge
Weighed down with well-thumbed romantic
Catherine Cookson novels
And she'll be dreaming as she always does.
And there's my nan's house
She'll be sat in her 'cubby hole'
By the black mantle grate.
Making the coals revamp
To boil a blackened kettle
And she will take an age to decide
Which teacosy will cover the pot today.
And there's the infirmary
Where my only son was born,
Where they said he may never walk in life,
Close by the old Adamsdown cemetery park
Where he did.
And a light rain is falling
That crystallises my stare
And there will be something missing
Now I'm not there.
All in passing by, all in passing by.
And I'm leaving the city
With its bulging briefcase full of cost
For somebody has to pay.

And my last thoughts are of bluebells
Glistening in the soft morning dew
Gathering them for my sick sweetheart
In the woods when I was a boy.
Climbing the white sanatorium wall,
Rushing to give them before they wilted
Into her small pretty hand

Then one day I came to call
Only to find neatly folded blankets
And an empty bed.

So I'm looking for
Where the wild bluebells grow
And where the blue is blue
Is that not a
'Leaving the city' thing to do?

Norman Royal

THE WAY BACK

On my shoes are marked many lonely miles, on my face the scars of sand,
I have shed the skin of a so-called life – you could never understand.
Why I chose to leave, to discover how, this huge cosmos came to be,
that I had to find all the reasons why, and a longing to be free.

So I left my life, living out the dream, of a man who lost his way,
to retrieve myself, reaching out to hope, not believing I could stray.
Hot deserted plains, unforgiving hills, where God's beasts created home,
I would stumble – fall, but resist the call, to return and never roam.

You can turn your back on your family and pretend you do not care,
give away your coin and security, like it really wasn't there,
Toss the compass up, watch it fall back down on a path that has no name,
just continue on, not a thought for those, you can let them take the blame.

But misguided souls can run out of steam and the world can call your bluff,
lonely days run cold, losing out on light, in the end it's not enough.
In my selfish heart ran a trace of love, like a river finds the sea,
I relinquished all but I still fell short and the dream was not to be.

In my shoes are marked many lonely miles, on my body, scars of sand,
I have shed the skin of a million years – you could never understand.

Hilary Kendrick

SUCH A SAGA IN A HAIR-CURL

Blonde hair's meant to be the passport to more fun
But curls are a Visa for women determined
To start good times rolling for them and their men.
The perm's a vintage item, invented when the last century was born, bathed and napkinned.
Think of yourself, madam, as a lady going into a hairdresser's to subject yourself to torment, by those fearsome tendrils dangling down
It's the weirdest contraption that ever came to town . . .
Just to transform sweet flossy locks to a ridged 'do'.
Those were the looks customers paid for, when coiffeurs did magic with unpromising tresses.
Through their doors maidens' despair came, but in an hour or two,
Our babes walked with as much pulling power
As exerted by hour-glass-figure dresses.

Gillian Fisher

CELEBRATING GETTING OLDER

Now I am retired I love the morning but not on a cold, wet Monday, the duvet seems to hold me
The alarm clock always seemed so urgent and loud, now I hear the gentle tick of the clock
I sometimes miss the wage packet reward but not the 7 o'clock traffic madness before me.
The day spreads ahead, time for me not as Mum, nurse or cook, time to write that book and take stock.
Life feels like a long meal, the starters being school, engaging in learning
The main in employment, now I am on dessert.
Children have grown and made a new life for themselves, always in my heart but no longer in my home
Like a beautiful tree growing tall and branching out, one day slow, the next day putting on a new spurt.
Time to clean that cupboard or shed, sort out the wardrobe but there is no time today, I have friends to phone.

Lying in my bed planning the life ahead, long plans seem challenging and changing, time to grow old disgracefully.
Pictures of my beautiful grandchildren drift before me like small dots of fairy dust, my bucket list is getting longer
I see the colours of day and night vibrant in my mind, Mother Nature outside my window dances gracefully
Time to add to the to do list, I hope my dodgy hips and knees hold out and get a little stronger.

June Witt

LOVE

Love makes you feel happy
Love is a destiny
Love is a secret
Love is nature
Love is someone's soulmate
Love is lucky
Love is free
Love makes you daydream
Love makes you feel warm
Love makes your heart beat
Love makes you smile
Love makes you feel that you are floating on air
Love makes you feel special
Love makes you feel wanted and loved
Love makes you excited
Love makes your eyes dilated
Love makes you sparkle
Love makes you tingle
Love makes your eyes light up
Love makes your face light up
Love makes you have goose bumps
Love makes your hair stand up on your skin
Love makes you feel nervous
Love gives you an energy rush
Love gives you an adrenaline rush
Love makes you attracted
Love gives you an energy rush
Love makes your heart beat fast
Love makes you feel you can do anything
Love can surprise you
Love can make you feel young
Love can come out of the blue
Love is instinct
Love is emotional
Love is a connection
Love is a feeling
Love is an aura
Love is a scent
Love is memory
Love is a smell
Love is for living
Love is for laughter
Love is for talking
Love is for kissing

Love is for hugging
Love is for crying
Love is for reading
Love is for touching
Love can make you melt
Love is romantic
Love is a best friend
Love is what you want to be
Love is what it can be
Love is a sign
Love is everywhere
Love is special
Love is a heart.

Lindsey Jane Way

THE ARCTIC IN THE SKY

I see some white clouds in the sky,
They look like icebergs gleaming high.
Lit from behind by the setting sun,
Which slowly sinks down, its daily course run,
I imagine the blue sky is water so cold,
Revealed as the ice melts in the sun shining gold.
One cloud seems shaped like a polar bear
But it's only a fantasy – nothing to fear.
It's just a reminder of last night's TV
And the sights near the North Pole for all to see.
Views of the world so far, far away
Which someone discovered on a journey one day.
He filmed what he saw to share it with others,
Who may never visit this place he discovered.
There are parts of our world which are freezing cold,
Or covered with forests in days of old.
And then there's great deserts unbearably hot,
And cities of concrete now cover a lot.
Wonders worldwide appear on our screens
With amazing sights which travellers have seen.
What would our ancestors of long, long ago
Think of the present? I really don't know.

Enid Hewitt

THE OCEAN AWAITS

An early morning shoreline scene
Anywhere on this world
Whether it be standing before
The rising sun or with it
Warming your back
As you gaze out across these waves
The ocean awaits

The ocean awaits
To take you on your life
From beyond these lands
From beyond these sands
Beyond the horizon
That you will never conquer
Yet always be in thrall of

And when you've reached
The far-off shores and tides
As your life begins to slow
And mortality claims its throne
You'll find yourself once more
Upon these early morning shores
The ocean awaits

The ocean awaits
To take you from this life
Far beyond these sands
Far beyond these sands
Beyond the horizon
That proves to be nothing more
Than a veil to a new existence.

Richard Gould

GRANDPARENTS

Grandad doesn't wear cardigans
He says the word belongs to a place in Wales.
He prefers a leather jacket, black, of course
To match the motorbike he rides
Nightly through his imagination
While Grandma makes cocoa and watches 'Come Dancing'

Grandma's a bit deaf, a bit daft
A bit lame, a bit slow
And one of the cleverest people in my universe.
She wouldn't know a PlayStation from a bus station
But she's always there to catch anything my mother drops
Either from hand or mouth

They confront and confound my perceptions of age
By not having been born, tired, at the age of sixty.
Grandad flew fighter planes and got medals for killing people
Grandma was torpedoed and watched her best friend get eaten by a shark
And now she drinks cocoa and he dreams of motorbikes
And the grandchildren think that's all they've ever been.

Martyn Carey

SAVE ME FROM YOUR LOVE

There you are, I see you there,
Don't be afraid, do not despair,
That was me, the woman in your dream that night,
Unafraid to step out of safety and into the light,
The woman who, according to you
Possessed an angel's complexion.
Out of sight, out of mind, perfect in every section,
The one with a touch of mystery, a touch of grace,
Elegance hidden behind every zip and lace,
Paintings fade but memories stay,
Why did you go and leave me this way?
Water is falling, the ground drenched in tears,
Remember that word you used? The centre of all your fears?
Death's tactics and cold embrace,
Claims his victims without a trace,
Now you remember me and all the things you said,
How about we change the future and you can save me instead?

Hayley Cordley

FOR THE FORGOTTEN SOULS

For hundreds of years you have locked us away
In institutions and prisons, and kept us out of view
Where no one can see us and no one can hear us
Because you're afraid we might be just like you.

And you organise your collections for all worthy causes
To placate your guilt for these things you have done
And you smile oh so sweetly as you hand out our pills
A few antidepressants are the cure for our ills
But they just block out the symptoms like a cloud blocks the sun.

Once we were imprisoned behind Bedlam's thick walls
Like performing seals, like chimpanzees in a zoo
You came and you watched and you teased and tormented
The depressed and the manic, the confused and demented
While secretly fearing it could happen to you.

And now we've got special homes and hospitals
And you say that we're treated with greater respect
And we're fed and we're drugged and we're kept clean and we're sectioned
We're kept under sedation and free from infection
Hermetically sealed but emotionally wrecked.

Oh can't you hear a small voice in the darkness
Like a robin that sings 'neath a street light's false moon?
I'm not a freak nor a moron, I'm a person like you
I feel and I see and I hear just like you
I don't understand all your medical phrases
Are they just part of a plot to confuse and to daze us?
Please explain to me clearly what's going on in my head
I don't understand a single thing that you've said.

They're closing the wards now, they say we must go.
'Care in the community' means they just don't want to know
And the weak and the helpless are locked away in our prisons
By a world that can't understand and a world that won't listen
Or left to lie in the gutter and to sleep out in the cold
Another cardboard box home in a cruel dead-end road.

And still you don't want to admit we exist
You still turn your heads and refuse to admit
That there's a problem among you that won't go away
But it's getting more serious every day.
And we're classed with the dregs of the human race
Mental illness is still thought a disgrace
So they make promises and hold meetings to decide on our fate
They claim their expenses and decide on a date

To hold the next meeting and to discuss the last one
And though a million words said, still nothing is done.
And the terrified girl still lives with her fears
And the lonely old man still walks alone through the night
While you all wring your hands and cry crocodile tears
And you say that you care, you sympathise with their plight.

That you feel for the lonely, that you weep for the depressed,
That you care for the lost and for the obsessed.
Then get out your handkerchief now, prepare to shed tears
For now is the time to realise that you see us.
We're not the invisible men – we're flesh and blood just like you
We're the forgotten souls, the untouchable few.
And as I'm leaving, there's just one thought in my brain.
If Jesus came back here, you'd probably say He was insane.

Trevor Leah

WILL THIS BE THE LAST TIME I SEE IRELAND?

Into the fluffy white clouds, drifting in blocks as snow drifts,
A silver plane ascends, hot tears, fast rolling over cheeks, salty taste on lip.
Patchwork fields of uneven shapes, multicoloured tones of every shade.
Golden wheat waves and glistens in the late summer sun.
Ginger full heads of barely long, fair, sharp prickled hair, upright in the breeze.
Soft, feathery blonde ears oats, make the memories sore to an earlier spring.
Diligently prepared ground, awaiting hand-sprinkling of the oats on that Good Friday long ago.
Spiritually for real, Man spreading seeds of bread,
Against the element he hopes and prays for a good harvest.
Fast flashes to the people we took for granted.
The grans and aunts, mums and dads and siblings in their plenty.
Loneliness was never in the frame, we left our native land to feel the meaning of that word and it hurts.
How the sight of the first snowdrop in spring, will transport you back to your first sighting beneath the variegated holy tree in Lissenhall.
Memory of daffodils beneath the horse chestnut in that lined avenue, bordered by the ditches of rhododendrons of every hue.
Red, purple, white and skinny blues
Should this be the last time I see Ireland, she is responsible for the fullness of my mind and heart.

Margaret Gleeson Spanos

RANDOM JOTTINGS OF A FATTISH LADY

I was a skinny little child –
Aunts called me 'sandfly' – drove me wild.
Today – upholstered comfort-wise –
I've come to terms with girth and size.

Teenage years in World War Two –
Rations slim – sweet treats were few –
Lack of fruit brought spotty years –
And oft was I reduced to tears.

My twenties – then a neat eight stone –
But never really skin and bone.
Then marriage, children, endless meals –
All mums know just how that feels.

Slow came the pounds as year by year
My expertise brought us good cheer.
I developed quite a knack for cooking –
In recipe books was always looking.

The trouble is – I'm very short,
And though I know I always ought
To watch with care and eat much less –
Inside there seems much emptiness!

That schoolgirl appetite – still there –
And even though I don't much care
To lunch off lettuce leaves and air –
I rather would be slim than stout –
Much easier to rush about.

Always speedy on my feet –
At running both my girls I'd beat.
Enjoyed to put them through their paces –
And I always won in mother's races.

Alas – arthritis setting in –
A family trait with kith and kin
Achey joints – an awful bore –
So – sit around a great deal more.

Keep off this and don't eat that –
Cut off every shred of fat –
The taste buds yearn – as in my youth –
I just don't care – and that's the truth!

Jacqueline Morris

LOVELY DORSET

Lanes and pathways cover our county,
Many towns so full of bounty;
Hills and dales spread far and wide,
Plenty of woodland for animals to hide.

The giant on the hillside at Cerne,
The tanks at Bovington, so great to learn;
The schools at Sherborne as good as could be,
The sea and sand at Weymouth just great to see.

The Georgian town of Blandford truly of the best,
The River Stour passes through, it never has a rest;
The coastal road to Bridport gives true remarkable views,
The Monkey World complex loved by children and adults too.

Some glorious views from Shaftsbury with Gold Hill really great,
To Corfe with glorious castle truly first rate;
Then Swanage with its railway offers many a real treat,
But Badbury Rings, for many folk, a nice place to meet.

Our county town of Dorchester offers great scope,
Hardy ever present and offering great hope;
For William Barnes the dialect will always attract,
And Lawrence of Arabia will keep the mind intact.

This glorious rural county available to all,
One day when travelling west you'll call;
To see and hear the rural treats that still remain,
We know that from a visit there is very much to gain.

John Paulley

FOCUS

With an ever-shifting double vision
You soon know what surreal means.
See a second cutglass vase arisen
To float to where a doorframe leans,
Two flower arrangements instead of one.
You know the true door's on the right.
On the left, most certainly there is none.
Doors open, vases slip from sight.
Flowers reappear across someone's face.
Behind blossom friend or stranger?
One figure, not two, now crosses the space
From that cutglass in no danger.
You shake hands and say, 'How nice to see you'
Concentrate . . . focus . . . keep one head in view.

C M Creedon

NIL NIL

As regular as clockwork my husband would go out
To his club – the Buffaloes, you've heard of them no doubt.
One evening, as the children slept, I made a cup of tea
And settled in an armchair to watch a programme on TV.
Something quite enjoyable I'd looked forward to all day,
And later he came home again and had the cheek to say,
'Ah – I'm just in time. The match is on,' and switched to BBC.
'Hey –I'm watching a film,' I said. 'Change it back!' He stared at me.
'It's the *big match.*' Heavy emphasis. I rose up from my chair
And stormed out to the kitchen. He called, 'While you're out there
Make me a sandwich will you? A cheese one would be nice.'
I paused, kettle in hand, and said in tones of ice
'You know where the food is kept, *you* make it.' No reply.
Oh, he's sulking now I thought, and gave a little sigh.
There was a principal at stake here; I couldn't back down now.
But, on the other hand, I didn't want a flaming row.
Although too tired to argue, I made tea and took it in;
He hadn't asked for that you see, and so he didn't win.
Not the sandwich though – I'm not that daft, and not his blooming slave
To wait on him hand, foot and finger, another sigh I gave.
What did I find? A lolling head, a snore. Oh it's pathetic!
If you want to know what I think – football is anaesthetic.

Josephine Price

NEDDY

While driving down the road one day, a sad sight came to me
A little donkey dappled grey, was tethered to a tree
His head hung low, no hope had he, his life was ebbing fast
Starved and beaten 'twas plain to see, his joy in life was past
A group of ruffians near at hand, had parked and settled there
A rascally and motley band, for him they had no care
I with their leader haggled for the sale of poor old Ned
Hungry, wet, bedraggled, he needed to be fed
Gently now we lifted him, into the back of our old van
It seemed his life was getting dim, so quickly home we ran
I put him in a little shed, a shelter warm and dry
Then spread some straw to make a bed on which poor Ned could lie
Some warm milk and a bowl of grain, I felt for him was best
Now sheltered from the wind and rain, I left him quiet to rest
Ere morning came I early rose, to see if all was right
And if poor starving Neddy had survived his first free night
I cuddled him and softly said, 'Dear Ned, please eat some food'
He gently nudged me with his head, as though he understood
The vet came daily with his bag of medicines and potions
Pills and tonics and clean rags, to bathe his sores with lotions
The weeks went by, and our dear Ned grew plump and had quite healed
I felt he now was ready to be taken out to field
I led him to a meadow bright, on the banks of the River Severn
He frisked and capered with delight, this was a donkey's heaven
I advertised and one day bought a charming donkey lady
She was exactly what I sought, and I named her little Maidie
I took her out to meet our Ned; his joy was great to see
He and Maidie soon were wed, and two turned into three
My story now comes to a close, in happiest harmony
With Maidie, Ned and little Rose, my donkey family.

Olive Woodhouse

KNOWN WAITING

Gazing unseeingly into the flames,
Resting, time drifting by, preoccupied
Then thoughts rushing in, on moments cast
Intruding, stopping me in my tracks
Slowly memories sharpening my mind
My recall of distant days, long past
Hanging in curtained silence, whilst now
Abruptly brought vividly to mind
Everything that happened then
The loss, grief, sorrow and anguish
The pain of not knowing, an enigma
You were so young, bright and warm
Such a pretty, loving daughter
Laughter ringing falsely here
Around my presence now, you were
So full of life, so open, caring
Where did you go and why?
I distinctly remember that dark cold night
Shivering at the thought
I buried my face in the soft gossamer wool scarf
Of yours, then staring into the night
The lights from the nearby houses
Danced in rain-fractured flight
I remember you left to visit a friend
My heart thuds as I recall the telephone
Ringing loudly later that evening
Your friend asked, 'Where is Jane?
Is she still with you?'
'No,' I said, 'She is with you isn't she?'
Oh god! I felt instantly sick
The impossible reality as slowly
The threads of time ran into morning
But still no Jane, where is she?
How long ago? It feels like yesterday
It is now seven years, where did they go?
Where are you? What happened?
No evidence, no sightings
Just an unsolved missing person file
Sitting in a police station gathering dust
Someone must know something, somewhere!
My beloved daughter, I feel so helpless
If only I knew I could cope
I could put this terrible emptiness behind me
I could start putting my life to rights

I want to believe you are alive
That you are well, happy, but I shiver
I can only visualise the worst
Whatever that may be
I wipe the tears from my eyes
With heavy heart I pick up my book
Gazing into the embers of the fire
I put another day of wondering to bed.

Susie Sullivan

THE FINAL TRAUMA

She moves as in slow motion,
Gasping as she comes suddenly to rest, with heart breaking,
Trauma awaking the grief that lies dormant in her aching breast.
Dark imaginings bode emptiness for her future life,
Like residue of scar tissue in a mind
Rife with tortured memories of golden days, once theirs,
Now gone forever into a black hole of obscurity.
She dreams of what might have been;
Suspended in the mist of borrowed time, with eyes beseeching,
Arms reaching out for something now irretrievable – sublime.
Jumbled reasonings drive the millstone of her crushed despair!
The slow, relentless turning of the wheel
Offers no repair for her ground-down emotions,
Stretched out as sand on a distant shore,
Awaiting confinement to the deepest oceans.
She grieves in silent agony!
Suffering the throes of inner pain with body tensing,
Mind dispensing thoughts that have no meaning in her muddled brain.
Distant thunder raises the spectre of his untimely death!
Formal platitudes turn her mind to the horror of his final breath
And to all it would deny her:
'With deep regret' . . . 'Have to inform you' . . . 'Tragic death'
Then the final trauma:
'Killed under enemy fire.'

Tony Reese

THE UNEXPLODED BOMB SAGA LONDON 1943

Coming home from the shelter one morning we saw
A sign that we'd all learned to dread,
Our street was roped off, a warden stood by
'You can't go down there,' the man said.

'I have to go home,' I protested
'My father I know is in bed,'
'We've knocked at all houses still standing
There's nobody in them,' he said.

'If my father can sleep through an air raid,
He wouldn't hear knocking,' I cried
'That bomb could go off any moment,
And your father's not there,' he replied.

By then I was inwardly shaking
I knew that my dad could be killed
I had to outwit this man somehow
My head with ideas became filled.

I remembered that there was a courtway
That came out at the end of our street,
I could get to it through the next turning,
I took off with wings on my feet.

I unlocked the door and raced up the stairs
Dad was blissfully snoring away
I shook him and pulled back the bedclothes,
'Get up Dad,' I cried, 'don't delay!'

'Whatever's the matter?' he grumbled,
And pulled up the covers once more
'For goodness sake Dad,' I yelled, 'get up,
There's a time bomb outside the front door!'

He suddenly grasped what was happening
And the gravity of the event,
I threw him his clothes, we dashed out of the house
Grabbing the dog as we went.

One leg in and one out of his trousers,
He tried to get dressed on the run,
Shirt over arm, braces dangling,
He was swearing and cursing the 'hun'.

We came into view of the warden,
'How *did* you get down there?' he cried
'I told you my father was in bed asleep
You wouldn't believe me,' I sighed.

The warden seemed quite agitated
He stared at Dad shaking his head
'I cannot believe you slept all through that noise,'
'You don't know my father,' I said.

More problems for us were beginning
We had to find somewhere to stay,
We split up and went to our own special friends
Who were happy to help in that way.

It was three weeks before we were let down our street
The mountains of rubble had grown
Our house was still standing – but only a shell,
The pathetic remains of our home!

Doris May Morgan

RIDING THE ROLLERS

The fishermen, at eventide,
Glided the foaming and fractious waters across,
Longing and dreaming e'er they could lay anchor;
Waves were their workplace, but they felt every moment, a keen sense of loss.
Home seemed far, far off, but this was a task to perform without rancor.
Sunset spun shades of roses –
Shimmering crimson, reflected on foam,
The fishers welcomed the tang,
Refreshed, a tonic for salt –
Smothered noses;

Indication, thank God, they sailed towards home.
Then there were nets and shoals of good food stuff –
The shadowy shore was abounding with fish.
Families waited at open wide doors;
Another journey accomplished – safety, according to wives' fervent wish.
'Hi Dad!' pipes a pint-size cherub – and supper's a-simmer, lights cheerfully shine –
A fisher embraces a child he adores.

Ruth Daviat

I AM HAPPY IN JESUS

I am happy in Jesus
I am trusting in His word Though shattered by the storms of life
I shall not fear
For He will see me through
He will walk with me
And He will talk with me
So why should I fear?
He tells me I am His own
And that He loved me so much that
He suffered and died in my place,
That I should live a victorious and
Happy life by His grace.
One day He is coming to take me to
His lovely home above
What a day that will be!
The rule is that I must humble myself
To walk with Him
He is the King of kings.
He reigns on high.
Leaving to go to that beautiful home
I can take nothing with me,
But I can send it on ahead.
I hear His voice saying,
'All this I have done for you,
What have you done for me?'
Yes! He loves me.
He tells me I must be faithful
And true to His word
To be His own.
He will take me by His hand
And lead me to the Promised Land.

Joy Wilson

PENFRIENDS

I found a penfriend in a paper
Now I sit and write a letter
At last I have finished it much later
Perhaps I could have written better

Then in the morning I will go
Off to the post box oh! So fast
The waiting time will go so slow
Happy I will be when I hear at last

I woke one morning very late
And wondered if I would hear from you
So excited I waited at the gate
Yes, a letter from my friend so new

It was nice, she liked my letter
She told me she lived by the sea
Now I hope I can write something better
But first I will make some tea

I will tell her our village is small
We have a school where children can play
A beautiful church but no shops at all
But a town that is not far away

I hope this friendship will last
As I have lots more things to tell
How the grandchildren are growing so fast
And all the great grandchildren as well.

Phyllis Nichols

HE KISS

When he was born and came home with his mother
We were afraid on our own to look after our treasure.
When he lay still in his cot we looked at each other
And gave him a kiss to check he was breathing.

He was just a small child that first day at school
Proudly we watched as he skipped with his friends up the lane.
And he never looked back nor saw the tears in our eyes
As we blew him a kiss from hearts full of pain.

And later he walked to the Cubs with his friend
Staying together and looking both ways at the kerb
Before crossing the road and then straight home at the end
Both going and coming too old for a kiss.

In his teens he loved going out on his bike
Up and away when he saw the sun rise.
He always was home before darkness to tell us
Where he had been. The kiss was in all our eyes.

When he started to drive he knew how we worried
And told us exactly where he would be.
He assured us that when driving he never hurried
Giving his mother a kiss before going to bed.

Until that night. We both looked at each other
When the clock struck eleven and our hearts turned cold
As we made excuses and turned the TV down
To hear the car come home. The kiss was on hold.

Minutes turned into hours and our feelings changed,
Telling each other he would soon be home
But increasingly angry because it was strange –
Bewildered and aching to give him a kiss.

Saying nothing we knew we would have to ask
How he could treat us like this after all we had done
And asking if the kisses meant nothing to him
When he knew how we worried until he came home.

The phone never rang. Lights went out all around.
Anger plotted how to deal with the boy. We dozed
On and off until the doorbell rang as daylight dawned
To silhouette a policeman standing in the porch.

We were shamed of our anger as we were told
That our precious son did all he could to miss
The speeding driver. But for hours he lay dead in a ditch.
And we were not there to give him his kiss.

Gerry Miller

FULFILLED

The time was ripe and Heaven sang
With words unknown before.
And the sun was born, in a
Crimson flood, with sparks from
The Earth's deep core.
Then the Lord spread stars
And silken scarves on the dark eyes
Of the sky – and the stars leaped
Up and twirled and sang as
The planets made reply.

From God's right hand the
Holy Word was thrown to spin
And fly – and He came with a shout
On an angel's back
Where mist had become
The sky. The Holy Word
Has strength and power to light
The birth of Man, the voice
Of God has blood and bones –
The Word becomes a Man.

Janet Harmer

SLOWLY LOSING MY MOTHER

I may never know how it feels to lose sight of all that is real
To forget what I remembered and remember what I knew
I can only offer an opinion
A very personal point of view
I felt pain like no other earlier today
When asked to introduce me I heard my mother say
'Of course I know who she is, it's my sister I'm sure'
But I'm her first born, a daughter, she doesn't remember anymore
This tale of loss has not been easy to begin
I stand on the outside helplessly looking in
It is only the sufferer that can attest to the frustration
Of memory loss experienced by an increasing part of the nation
How do I describe losing a living breathing soul?
A person who thinks I am a visitor
A woman who no longer has goals
It is hard to watch this thief of life
As it nibbles viciously at her mind
Swallowing every vestige of sanity and joy
Removing thoughts of her girl and her boys
Most of us fret when we lose a key or our phone
Imagine not knowing your way back home
Trapped within an invisible cage
Frustration fuelling an inner rage
Fingers ever moving, body never still
We love you Mum and we always will
Many beautiful things complete our lives
Pain has carved a place on the face of my father
At the slow disappearance of his wife
So I mourn whilst the life is still living
Day after day I watch as the changes occur
I hope for a miracle and return to normality
Not for me you understand, but for her
There are occasional periods of lucidity
When the hurt and confusion shine bright in her eyes
But no matter how arduous the journey
I will never move far from her side
For this is the person who ensured my safety
Gave me guidance in times of stress and pain
The least I can do for my parents
Is make sure they receive the same.

Lynn Elizabeth Noone

44

REFLECTIONS OF A LATE-NIGHT JUNKIE

If only I could have the chance to live my short life again
I'd save my family the grief and save myself the pain,
But it's too near the end of it now . . . my strength is fading fast
As I lie here reflecting on my sad and lurid past.

In my childhood things were normal and I enjoyed the pursuits of youth
But as a teen I got into trouble, now I must tell the honest truth,
I refused to listen to my parents or treat them with due respect
So I started getting into trouble . . . what else could I expect?

We just hung around the streets at night feeling bored with nought to do
Quite soon I became a petty thief as I'd started sniffing glue
None of us had any jobs because of chronic unemployment
Crime seemed the best way to get our kicks . . . our cheap enjoyment.

At first we felt we were in complete control until we started to inject
Now we were on the downward path and soon lost all self-respect
The next few years passed in a mist. I scarcely can recall
Sometimes high but more often low . . . life made no sense at all.

Running wild, stealing, vandalising were our favourite types of fun
My family were devastated as I was their only son,
Where is that life I've never had? Once I was really smart and keen
To go to university and become a doctor . . . I am still only nineteen.

I am dying now and I'm so scared . . . My sight is already bad
I caught AIDS from dirty needles as we shared everything we had,
I will skip the gory details, I caught this disease through my own fault
It's too late when you do get hooked and without help you cannot halt.

There is no point in crying or saying that I was easily led
It doesn't matter now for me as I will soon be dead.
Do not dabble at all if you've any sense . . . We did but we were mugs
I will soon be just a statistic . . . 'Another death by drugs!'

I will make this final plan now before I leave this Earth
Listen to me . . . You will kill yourself . . . avoid drugs for all you're worth
I would not wish this terrible disease on my worst enemy
Learn a lesson from my experiences . . . Heed this last warning from me!

Mary Anne Scott

BUILDING UP, BUILDING DOWN

I speak to the spirit of the building,
To the vibrance of what is past;
To the echoes of voices, like infra-red pictures,
Tracing centuries of brick and human warmth
And I join in the shuddering, the painful rending
Of metal against metal, bone against bone,
As the last, succulent pieces of cement
Twist on sinew in the late afternoon sun.

The foreman, burning tobacco, offers no libation,
No apology to you, oh building, for services past;
While the thurible of metal swings and swings,
Becoming the destruction bird, pecking
Like a carrion crow, at the eyes
That drop away sadly, glinting with last thoughts
In the dying pyre of dust, signaling back
To the overseeing sun.

Here you housed many generations;
Here you gave work to many.
My people, what have I done to you?
Answer me.

I speak to the spirit of the building,
To the charnel house of evening fires.
I speak to the graveside, the neat piles
Of wood and brick; the small, small mounds
And I join in the sorrow of the wind
With the eddies and gusts of last being.

At the resurrection I wonder
How, in the shortness of night hours,
The new tenants stand the minute voices
Of what has been, whispering through the blocks
Of pre-stressed concrete, 'I was a brick.'
'I was the cornerstone. Listen to my voice.'

'As you are, so I was. I joyed at the sun;
Filled my hours with people; held them at night
Against storm and rain. Listen to me,
For I, and my end will come, again and again.'

Michael Vipond

BUTTONS

I loved the tin of buttons when I was just a kid,
It sat up high on the kitchen shelf showing off its lid,
The countless buttons it contained were magic in our fingers
We sorted them in colours and for hours we would linger . . .

The collection was a huge one salvaged from old clothes,
Jumble sales and hand me downs, buttons would be hoved.
It was a very busy tin that Mam would often use
Replacing and completing the clothes we did abuse . . .

The memories are made of bliss, Mam taught us how to count
On the kitchen table, colours and pictures we would account.
We played games like shopping and swapping different sizes
Taught us many values in all sorts of guises . . .

When air raids hit in the war, a safe place we would find
Mam always bringing up the rear with the tin intact behind
Neighbour's boyfriend losing button off his trouser flies,
Panic soon averted before things went awry . . .

As we all got older, the good old button tin
Often came in handy changing buttons on a whim,
The garment would be proudly worn, almost good as new
Changing buttons was a gift, we swapped them quite a few . . .

In later years my children loved it just as much as me,
I kept it sat on my kitchen shelf for one and all to see
Well-used and revered by all who knew its history
Kids and grandkids used it as an abacus of mystery.

I love that tin of memories, but don't ask me how many
Various buttons it contains, they are more precious than money . . .

M L Damsell

FIGHT

I finally believe I've found a way to say
All the things that cross my mind
Consuming my thoughts
Darkening my sight
My head is full of nightmares even in the brightest light.
I fight the good fight. Fight for my life.
But when I'm bound and chained and penned in a cage of fear and doubt with no way out . . .
How can I see the light and the best way it could turn out?

And there are people to turn to,
People who've learned this shit the hard way too!
But what's the age-old advice they give to you?
'Carry on regardless.' Don't you know what that asks of us?
The greatest task since Noah built that bloody ark!
Don't give me that lark.

But you can't be blamed,
You've played life's game and are loved for it;
And there's not much to say because each individual's life will turn out its own way.
I'm still waiting to pave mine, but in time I'll find the reason and rhyme
The way to get out and get on and see something through
The lens of defeat and snatch the victory through effort and desire to leave something behind
So I know I wisely spent my time.
And on that note, as the flow slows . . .
I think I'll go.

Joshua Barnard

ATTEN-SHUN

Corral the carnage in regimented rows
Of shining blinding stone.
Cover mud-caked khaki
With sweet lavender and rose.
Bring order from chaos,
Light to fields made dark
By gas and shells and arid smoke.
Lay friend and foe in line,
No nationhood beyond the grave.
You help us mourn and honour their names
But only our hearts can grasp the pain.

Pat Andrews

THE NATURE OF THINGS

When you long for the sun, on a cold winter's day,
And look at the sky, so cloudy and grey,
Think of tomorrow, and the joy it can bring,
And remember my love, it is the nature of things.

When you hear on the wind, the curlew's cry,
With warm setting sun, painting red all the sky,
Look at the sight, with the beauty it brings,
And remember my love, it is the nature of things.

As you look at the sea, while waves reach the shore,
With white surf swirling, every nook to explore,
Seagulls above, on sleek graceful wings,
Remember my love, it is the nature of things.

On a walk through the woods, where tall pines grow,
When you are feeling down, with your spirits low,
Look at the trees, and the joy they can bring,
And remember my love, it is the nature of things.

As you glance at the sky, on a clear summer's night,
Watching the stars, twinkling so bright,
With moon casting shadows, on ivy that clings
Remember my love, it is the nature of things.

When you think of the loved ones, whom you have lost,
The night is so cold, and ground thick with frost,
You listen to a baby's first cry, all the wonder it brings,
Remember my love, it is the nature of things.

When you feel sad, at the end of the day,
You are missing your loved one, so far away,
Think of each other, and the joy it can bring,
And remember my love, it is the nature of things.

Jim Wilson

49

PAPER JEWELS

Tomorrow I shall have to tell them.

Gone are the diamonds
Red glittering jewels,
Golden dress,
Paper money.

My soul is never empty.

Gone is the white stallion,
Heaven's dance,
I'll not taste Satan's feast,
Pink sweetmeats.

My God is with me.

Gone is the talk of love,
Echoes of laughter,
My last life.

Do not chastise me.

This Muslim girl
Speaks truth.

Only salt tears will fall.

Tomorrow.

Mary Mullett

THE BOATMAN

The boatman of the ferry boat has never grown up.
He imagines paper boats running down the stream,
Foreign crafts, carried safely to some strange land.
The sun climbs in the sky and he is happy.

The boatman of the ferry boat knows about growing up,
Having steered many stupid courses uselessly laden.
Playmate clouds hide the sun only to let it peep
On the rivulets of seas crossing the memory.

The boatman of the ferry boat has chosen never to grow up,
Because he chooses to sail the waters that swim his thoughts,
As brother and sister bathe and play on the banks of his dreams
Strong and secure and laughing, safe in a mother's love.

Ivy Bates

FLY ON THE WALL

You cannot see me
I'm up high
I'm so free
And I can fly

You're so clear
From my high view
No need to fear
I can't hurt you

If you could see me
You would sigh
Grab something
To make me die

But out the window
Out of sight
I'm much too quick
And I've got height

Another window
In I go
To perch and buzz
It thrills me so

What fuss you make
When me you spy
Upon your ceiling
Way up high

Your secret's safe
I will not tell
I cannot speak
Your lives of hell

I'm just an insect
Passing by
I notice things
Then fly on by.

Sonia Richards

THE GODDESS

The room is dark
Yet in a second is filled with light
A vision appears, a goddess ethereal
Clothed in a gown of shimmering white
Her hair is bronze and in abundance
Falls to her waist, ending in coils below her knees.
Her eyes are topaz blue
Piercing and very bright
Her face is soft and translucent white,
I reach out, I want to touch,
Fire within me lights.
Desire, passion, and to fulfill my needs
Alas, alas, it was not to be
As she appeared, she disappeared from me
Who was she? I do not know
Where she came from I cannot go
All I hope, if I am given time
She may appear, and tell me who she is
Why was I chosen
To see her at this time?

Carl Kemper

BYE-BYE BLISSFULNESS

Beautiful blushing bride Belinda
(Blue bra borrowed.)
Bashful bridesmaids Beverly, Beth
Both besotted by Bobby,
Brilliant banquet, best bubbly, bonnie bouquets,
Badly behaved bell boys battle,
Boozers brawl,
Betty, Bridget, Bertha,
Bitch behind backs,
Big, bloated Bernadette burps,
Band blasts blues,
Bruce, Boris, bond, become buddies,
Brother Billy blabbers
Bridegroom Brian's been bonking brothel babes,
Blazing bride Belinda blubbers,
Bloody B – Bloody B – Bloody B.

Peter Yates

NOVEMBER

Early darkness,
Veils of mist in cold air.
The trees stand silent
Against a mournful sky
In its triste melancholy.
The rain is falling
On a damp, soggy earth
Preparing for winter's sleep
As it has done in eternal mystery
For millions of years
Of birth-death-rebirth.
One feels such awe – yet such a void!
A sadness deep down – tearless,
Who is lonely now,
Is in need of tender hugs.
Who is homeless now,
Should know of a loving heart.
Who does feel unloved
Should look toward Heaven!
And yet – a candle is burning
In longing human hearts and souls.
A light never to go out!
A light – called *hope*.

Hans Richter

UNTITLED

I
Do try
To be positive
And aim to live
Keeping an open, alert mind
Leaving bigotry and lies far behind
Nourishing hopes, planning for the future,
Welcoming the chance for adventure,
Never without a book
Or resolute outlook
To remain
Sane.

Sheila Dodwell

ELITE

They say life is tough at the top
Yet you're free from physical pain
And at the top of your game
Money flows in like Niagara
You don't need to use Viagra
Women throw themselves at you
Attracted by magnetic charisma and charm
But often you need help from a health farm
Gifts given to only a few
The elite where the greats of life meet
You excelled at school, sporty, the lot
They say life is tough at the top
Played piano like Brahms at the age of six
Yet you suffer from depression and need an uplifting fix
But victory was your only aim
You've achieved so much but act like one who's lame
I understand it's boiling the pressure
Do this, do that, pushed here, pulled there
Like rock bottom expectations are there
It's confusing with every camera that goes pop
It's pressure, it's rough, it's judgmental at top
When you feel down
False friends don't want to hang around
Ali, Elvis, Lennon, Lincoln
Nelson, Jesus, Gandhi you're with them
You've left a mark on civilisation
The confusing thing is what to do next.

John Beals

ONLY LOVE CAN MOVE MOUNTAINS

A smile can turn winter into spring,
Teach an elephant to sing,
And convince a camel he is king –
But only love can move mountains.

A gentle word can bring out the sun,
Send the devil on the run,
And turn a crocodile into a nun –
But only love can move mountains.

A kiss can turn a cabbage gold,
Make a craven coward bold,
And change an angel into a scold –
But only love can move mountains.

A loving hug can turn black white,
Make a slimy slug take flight,
And change the daytime into night –
But only love can move mountains.

Mary Baird Hammond

JUBILEE

We are told
Heaven is a lovely place
But nobody seems
In a hurry to get there

Clouds like cumulus
Like wandering sheep
Like galleons at full sail
Like cotton wool
Like crocodiles sleeping in a blue pool
Like angels' wings
Like puffs of smoke
Like mares' tails
Like love spools

Like ice flows
Drift across the sky
Heaven was yesterday.

Frances Jessup

THE TRANSPORTATION SECURITY ADMINISTRATION

It is September 2001 just before the fall
I'm in Central Park on a burger stall
Some say opportunity appears by the day
There's a chance for me in the TSA

Back home Mama says, 'Don't be a fool
For a job like that you'd need more school'
I says, 'Mama you know I'm ever so smart
Don't I feed you all from my burger cart?'

I gets me a form and sends it away
I wait for the mail, an answer to say
In no time at all, just a week to the day
I'm to RV at DC for the TSA

At the centre of power, Washington DC
I'm one of a group of 10,000 and three
No burgers, mustard or cold winter nights
It's JFK, NY and thousands of flights

There's Cortez from Phoenix, and Murphy from Cork
Hans from Bavaria and Ahmed the Turk
Men from Seattle who can't even sleep
And three from Texas who arrived in a jeep

There are ones from the Rockies and some from the plain
A Chicago hood and an Indian from Maine
You'll read this and wonder with awful dismay
Could this shower be recruited in the TSA

After recruiting, selection and even induction
We get to an airport, we'll cause such a ruction
We're the pride of the crop and all have to say
May God help the public from the TS of A

You stand up and answer and don't take the mick
We're Federal Officials so don't give us no stick
Our orders, we know, they don't make any sense
To refuse to obey is a Federal Offence

Don't bother to use the locks we approve
We'll cut them off anyway, it's such a smart move
We rummage in cases, bags and computers
And cause maximum chaos to all the commuters

This tale of valour, and courage and grit
Hassle foreigners and frisk the odd Brit
In the war against terror, what was your work?
I served in the frontline, JFK in New York.

William Brown

DEAR WORLD

Dear world, you really have messed it all up
Not once but again and again
The faults you have made like a giant cascade
Have fallen upon us like rain

The weather went haywire long, long ago
The finance, dear world, has gone mad
There are now more criminals outside jail
Than in, and that really is sad

Where are the good old days we once had?
How did you get it so wrong?
With poor people suffering more and more
And rich people banging the gong

Sweet family life has gone down the drain
With love and respect shown no more
They all want more money, and wealth but no work
It's not like it was before

Blank out the sunshine, switch off the moon
Thank goodness you cannot do that
Us wise ones have pulled up the drawbridge
The idiot, is under your hat.

John Robert Burr

GOLDEN HOURS

Such beauty in a summer's day,
When birds awake in dawn's display
Whilst stars so gently fade away
And colours riotously splay
Across the sky at break of day.
Clouds soft and delicate as lace,
Weave patterns overhead embrace,
Our guardian angel friends who grace
In shining raiments light as lace.
Heavenly blue and verdant green
Goldfinches charming rest and preen,
Bees seek choice honey for their queen,
Whilst sunbeams gild and slide between
The trees and shrubs of evergreen.
Golden moments, sunshine hours,
Coolness in the scented bowers,
Rainbows glowing, summer showers,
Colours brightly tinting flowers,
Memories in tranquil hours.

Lorna Troop

RAGE STANDS

Rage stands in the corners of every urban street,
Kicking its feet, raising its fist
Like birds caged in their rusty cages
Covered with dirt and filth
Wings clipped, never able to fly and raise themselves above the working class necropolis
The underclasses, the walking dead eyes set to the dead
Sunset needles stuck in every vein
Just no futures, no stages
Just theatres of urban wars,
Fighting not for liberty or freedom but just to feed the mouths of children
Throwing dummies to the floor
Sodden with urine and blood
May the angels cry their wings broken too,
Because in Heaven they all eat with plastic spoons
Sitting on crate boxes
The souls of the greedy and the souls of the bankers.

Natalie Brookes

58

THE GOOD LIFE

It is nice to sit alone with good things on your mind,
Of special people in life who care for you and are so kind,
My little dog Ruby sits by my side
She often is naughty then runs away and hides.
Such good friendship that I share,
People who I have met and I show how much I care,
My best friend drives a taxi for a living
She is so wonderful like me, kind and giving.
My husband loves to play bowls,
We all celebrate when England score their goals.
Life is so good, in fact it is great,
To have love and laughter and I cannot wait,
For now I am nearly fifty years old
I have a wonderful life
And in my heart and arms
My favourite people I hold.

Sally Warren

WORD FOR WORD

Words are funny creatures
If you think of it a while
Some are very powerful
While others have some style.
The ones that are important
Are the ones that connect each word.
To help the reader understand
All they have read and heard
The number of letters in one word
Differs as you know
When we are young and need to learn
We look at words, they help us grow
To understand the meaning of the human word
Is quite a feat I grant you
Words can bring us close together
So words I want to thank you.

Julie Valente

THE DOG CALLED TESSA

Outside the library, John and me,
We met a woman with a puppy,
I went to stroke its little paws,
Tessa got up on all fours.
To our surprise as John said, 'Hi'
The puppy replied, 'I am fine.'
'How do you do? The two of you?'
She said all this, I swear it's true
Young Tessa was a polite thing,
With no loud bark for a greeting,
Tessa could talk like me and you,
So try with your dog, it might talk too.

Tracey Anne Barrett

MAKING SENSE

Afraid that lines mean what they say,
That the sound words make is exactly that.
No underlying subtlety, no ulterior other
Than what appears to be.
Metaphor to illumine a phrase,
To make it sharp and clear
And not cloak with mystery.
Alliterate to highlight and stress
The rhyme and rhythm.
A nudge to the memory,
A hook to latch onto a fleeting fancy.
A thread of reason winding in and out
Behind the ordered humdrum of day-to-day
Meditation needs a cloister, guarded from
A busy brain listing and plotting and living,
Anxious to leech into quiet, to edge into peace.
Easy to let boundaries blur. Harder to listen
To that still, small voice trying to make sense
Of why tentative reaches for comprehension
Can be grasped and turned into certainties
And dogma, which does not answer the purpose.

Jean Greenall

60

HE SOLDIER

A raindrop fell upon
The petals of a flower
A delicate silken rose
Sheltered within a shady bower.
A teardrop fell upon
Her white satin gown.
It slid slowly downwards
And splashed into the ground.
Time for the regiment to move
'Twas the moment of farewell
He handed her a rose bud
Then strode out towards Hell.
Raindrops fell on rose petals
Teardrops fell on her satin gown.
They mingled close together
Then lay buried in the ground.
She heard the sombre toll
Of the solitary chapel bell
It masked the sound of gunfire
As he strode valiantly into Hell.

M Elizabeth Workman

HOME FROM THE MUD
(Dedicated to those of the Somme)

Then the sun shone, through a slit between the curtains,
Shining brightly, like a beam from Heaven.
No more bombs and bullets,
No more over the top we go.
But a sweet caressing light,
Over an eiderdowned bed, with prospects,
For such a day,
To walk down well loved paths,
And known ways.
Greeted by name, with a cheerful smile,
To look back to those days, not so far away
And remember well,
The friends and comrades we left behind
To guard our efforts,
A memorial, for all time.

Roy Anthony Rudham

SEVEN BROOKS

One of the seven brooks that cross our once quaint old town
Runs from the great lake, cascading down the falls onto the rocks below.
It passes the old Pretoria mine where 344 men and boys lost their lives.
The brook seems to swell as it meanders on by, some folk say with tears in their eyes.
Trapped down below all those years ago.

The brook runs alongside a forgotten footpath,
Before exploding into my secret garden.
Once inside it feels as though you have stepped back in time with rhyme 'n' reason,
Your thoughts take you through every season.

Sitting alone in my garden in spring,
Listening to the early songbird sing.
Hidden from view of prying eyes
Apple blossom trees blot out the bright sunlit sky.

Summer's now here, the brook looks divine,
Fishing for sticklebacks in the warm sunshine.
In the cool mountain stream I paddle my feet,
Rabbits at play within easy reach.

The autumn leaves of golden and brown,
Fall gently to the ground.
The hedgehogs and squirrels hurry to fill up their larders.
In winter they will find life much harder.

Winter comes along and my garden's now bare.
The brook's now a raging torrent, but it won't notice me as it sweeps out to sea.
A robin now flies into my tree, there are a few berries left for a friend oh so true,
I can't understand why he stays to see winter through!

I'll be back early next year, for it's my time well spent.
In my secret haven,
On the edge of dear old Chowbent.

Kenneth Pendlebury

GIRL ON A BICYCLE

She used to have
An old black shoogly bike
That she rode, fast as time
With hands, without hands, through hedges
Standing up on the pedals
To stop time rushing past.
And then to the other side of the hill
Hair streaming into the wind
Fast as Einstein's bullet
Arriving before she'd left.

But at the bottom of the hill
Time pooled.
And for a while, she drifted
Like a small unstrung balloon.
Until she began to walk, with measured step
One child cradled in her arm
The other held tightly by the hand.
And then the children, changed and grew
And climbed down from her tight held grip.
Running circles, spinning like coins
Pushing time on.

And soon the filling of plastic bags
Became a daily sport
With long stops, made for reflection
And tea
And what is known as, passing the day,
Yet, sometimes resting on that downwards slope
Her bags abandoned on the street
She's sure she hears the shriek of brakes
The hiss of wheels, the tug of wind
And almost tastes the salt of flying hair.
And wonders when she'll catch up with
The girl she left behind.

Pat Mackenzie

LOVE'S COURSES

No! Like a red rose love is not! That's just poetic trash
I can't describe it easily; a sort of, well mishmash.

It's much more like a vast repast which comes in several courses
And we are told that courses need specific sorts of horses.

Exampled thus, when at hors d'oeuvre I was skittish colt;
I'd get up to some mischief and then I'd do a bolt.

The soup was most enjoyable, a hunter bold was I;
My appetite was like a pain when a filly sauntered nigh

All through the meats, like a great big shire I plodded docile, true
And rushing up to fences was a thing I didn't do.

The nuts and port were comforting for Dobbin, out to grass
She stroked me with her curry-comb as I drained a brandy glass.

The banquet now seems cleared away; the knacker's yard is looming,
Finished are the munching, quaffing, prancing and the grooming.

Ended, all the foaling, snorting, rolling in the dew;
Gobbled, all the savouries, the fruits and ices too.

Now, see my poor old tattered tail, my head so sadly hung,
My quarters all quite atrophied, my withers sorely wrung.

Love endeth here, or so I thought in my erroneous fashion
But stubbornly it still persists with prefixing 'passion'.

Yes, love still peeps out of her eyes; she snuggles close to me;
I'll take just one Bath Oliver and dunk it in my tea.

Frank Sutton

PALE RIDER

When you read between the lines
And see the warning signs,
Then think warily on me
For I'm the passing of the times.

Like the wrinkles in my skin
And the shortness of my breath,
In all the places that I've been
I'm the bony face of death.

Today, what moves between the trees
Isn't only gentle breeze,
What rustles through the limes
Is the passing of the times.

As the cards pile one on one
In your Cassandraic fun,
Know you can't forever run
From the bony face of death.

You'll look back upon your crimes,
Hear the tolling of the chimes
And remember in your rhymes
The passing of the times.

Though you laugh away your days
In a hedonistic haze,
Know surely that you'll gaze
On the bony face of death.

So take care to do to others
As you would they'd do to you
And remember
At the passing of your time,
The only coin to buy respite
From the bony face of death
Is the mercy that you've shown
To lives not started yet.

Jim Rogerson

MALE

(A poem on the Maldivian capital)

Streets with no names
Joined onto nameless alleyways
Gullies and slip roads,
With unrecognisable features
Locals harbour stares of intrigue
As two Westernised figures
Puncture a pseudo-Westernised capital.
We walk, as hundreds of helmetless
Motorcycle riders fly;
Their nonchalant grip on the
Accelerator unfazed by vehicles
Inched away from a collision.
Malé has been built skyward
The population explosion
Paving the way for multi-storey
Housing faculties dwarfing
Rows of commercial outlets
Selling the latest technology.
Every space is used, homes
Stuffed in unseen crevices
Ramshackle, collections of bricks
Jammed into pin-sized holes.
Passing a divot in the road,
We observe quick repair work;
Bricks held in place by bricks
Fix it. Leave it.

A café by the Indian Ocean
Serves us mango flavoured
Iced coffee as we observe
Pockets of rubbish grabbed
And taken by the waves
Rippling up the artificial beach.
The non-existence of litter bins
Creates culminating mountains
Plastic bottles floating like buoys
Crisp packets left to spiral and dance
With occasional wisps of air.

Amongst the humidity are
Opportunities for momentary bliss
Restaurants, cafes and supermarkets
Containing skin-cooling air conditioning.
With drying throat and parched skin

Circulatory air spins around arm hairs
Sensationally reprieving the sweat.
We purchase one bottle of water
At five rufiyaa, we relax.
However, eavesdropping on
The conversation of a shop assistant
We come to notice how little
Of the local tongue we have learned
English words dropped in
Like coins in a piggy bank, but
Used sparingly and infrequently.
Nevertheless, the waitress' transition
Between Dvehi and English is effortless
Like a mating of swans.

Moving through the fish market
The hubbub of activity cascades
In fixating our eyes on tuna
The size of a human baby
Its fattened mouth hooked fast
From the corrugated iron roof
Tiddlers the size of coins,
Wrestling to jump over one another
In a watering can-come-bucket
A sailfish's lumpy head
Slammed down on the metal counter
Being relieved of its outer body.
Slashed by a machete blade
Into sizable and resellable chunks.

The night market is enriched
By the blasting cacophony
Of 90s style British pop.
Unseen boomboxes pumping
Out splurges of cringe-worthy sounds
Like ants the locals purchase numerous
Brooms, goldfish in transparent bags,
Multicoloured chicks (used as curiosities,
Disposable and dispensable balls of fluff)
And other pointless paraphernalia.

As we trundle back to our box-sized
Hotel room, the welcoming stench of
Unclean water enters our nostrils and
Our consciousnesses accept the
Unused traffic light, bent around The railings like a frog's leg.

Michael J Good

EARTH RUN RED

Watch those places you're walking,
Mind the way they talk
Watch out for people who sneak up in the dark
Watch out for the man with the gun who claims that he is smart
Bullets and bombs breaking all our hearts
The Earth is running red
With the violence and the dead
They will leave us dead Earth run red
We can't put our trust in no man
Not even a politician
Which is a true religion?

Take a good look in the mirror and tell me
Do you like what you see?
Masters of deception, corruption and evil
But you're always quick to point the finger at me
Won't somebody tell me?
I just don't understand the ways of the world today
Sometimes I feel like there's nothing to live for
So I'm longing for the days of yesterday.

Time is getting short, best find something to do
Think it would be wiser, if we helped each other too
I get up every day and the government, too chatty, chatty
Say one thing in our ear, twist then take it back,
We need to stop the things we know, know,
Take care of our lives, they're not for rent
There's nothing left to say,
But if you search deep enough in your soul
You'll always find the strength to carry on and see
'Won't somebody help me?'

Chelsea Henderson

FAITH?

It is not a singular thought that creates
But more a spinster of a godless life which
Lubricates the whirling pool of afterbirth for
Us to contend with
And froth and drown and frown and crown
Ourselves with a wounding of a bruised apple core.
A peach would rot finer and smell like a crime
But an apple decomposes quicker when chopped in two
Which one are you? May I ask as a man in the image of God?
Who must laugh and prance at my last line.
That is fine,
The cow did moo and sheep baa
As men came bearing gifts from afar
To a funnel web of thoughts and short
Lives printed in dusty old books
With looks that grow older and
Sometimes bolder with a diseased heart
And cancer.

Who chooses us to write?
On what subject under what fight?
A feigned retreat is steep in life,
To break insecurity
From darkness to light –

We never fashion or ration ourselves to one life
The world was spinning before you rose your
Head and will be turning when you are dead;
Until you grow tired of loitering with intent
In the under swirl.
Are you whole or chopped in two?
As the cleaved apple did grapple with the parting of seas.
Life determined by short staggered prayers between
Breeze block buildings and time unspent?
For some would rather die in battle than old cattle, prodded and poked on the doctor's table
Some gift to science or a God of fable.
Which path are you?
Are you whole or chopped in two?

Stuart Springthorpe

NO! TO THE EURO

I was born in the year nineteen forty-four
When my country England was still at war
Being an island surrounded by sea
Saved us then from the slavery of Hitler's Germany.
It took us sixty years to repay the loan, begrudgingly given by American businessmen
That money enabled my people to continue the fight for freedom and our country to defend.
In recent years, the then prime minister Tony Blair involved us in a distant war
Getting our country to back America, 'What for?'
He told President Bush, 'We'll back you all the way'
Didn't ask the British people to have their say.
Eurocrats are trying to dictate terms over the Euro
Thank goodness we did not adopt it, due to the market's down turn, we're still on the borrow
Our banks are given billions of tax payers' money
Then resist giving the man in the street a decent loan, acting like bees hoarding honey
The money would be better invested in industry and building construction if given
To get the men back to work and earning a living
Plumbers, joiners, bricklayers etc, getting their taxes paid
If new homes won't sell, then rent them out, so the path to economic recovery is laid
The government has no money of its own
It's money from workers hard work and taxes from which our country has grown
Those in power are making cuts on the people which is mean
Stop giving free handouts to non tax payers not entitled to a benefit scheme
In the past we've been encouraged to live beyond our means
Some countries can no longer pay their debts, so it seems
For them there's no work, no money and some have lost their homes
They keep having to ask Germany for extra loans
The government here are afraid on Europe, to let the people vote
Knowing we don't want to follow the Euro down its slippery slope
For those other countries I am deeply sad
But for us being stubborn and fairly independent, I'm glad
We can no longer help other countries out
Charity begins at home, getting back on the economic track is what it's all about
The people in Britain have tightened their belts enough
The government should stop measures that harass the people making things tough
Economists say it'll be years before the end of the downturn is in sight
But if there are jobs for people, at the end of the tunnel there will be a light.

Ann McAreavey

YOU WAIT, WE WAIT

It's such a shame you've
got the weight of the world
on your young shoulders
and there's boulders in your
way
'cause the road's not straight.

You wait, silently you wait
for the faraway horizon
to walk towards you but,
deep down you know that
just won't happen.

An' snapping, snapping are
the dogs at your heels
sure is hard to be brave
when you know how it feels
an' you never had a dream
come true
you said it wasn't up to you.

Yes here comes the heavy rain
and it's dark and you're alone
in an empty street
nothing to do, nowhere to go, no –
one to meet
and the dead of night seems
to hold no light for you.

Still here comes the sunrise
and it wants to take a shine
to you
it's true.

It's such a shame you've
got the weight of the world
on your shoulders
maybe today there'll be less
boulders in your way and
the road will be more straight
we'll wait and see.

Rowan Wallis

THE RED KITE · (THE SPIRIT OF THE GODDESS ISIS)

I glanced upwards, towards the heavens,
And there she was,
Flying in a circle of pure unbroken love,
Her wings outstretched in a symmetrical silhouette of pure perfection,
Flying within the deepness, of the beautiful lapis sky.
She filled my heart with such love,
I could see her with my eyes,
And feel her in my soul.
She pervaded my every being.
She ventured across the sun,
The beams filtered through the tips of her wings,
Streaming down into my heart, like strands of the finest gold,
Filling my heart with a precious golden light,
Her breath igniting the flame of my heart,
Each breath, allowing the flame to burn with ardent fervor.
I felt her breath on the nape of my neck,
Her spirit entered the portal of my soul,
Her love and protection, enveloping me, in fiery but gentle passion.
All consuming, all powerful, all beautiful.
The moment seemed to last forever,
Then I looked up, and she was gone,
Leaving my heart aflame,
Burning brightly with her love, her protection and her passion,
She left me feeling, that it was almost as if we were one,
Connected by pure love, floating in the cosmic serenity of a lapis blue sky.

Corinda Daw

TO A DISH CLOTH

Oh simple friend that lies so happy there
Between the palm of this industrious hand
And swishing through the waters soapy depths
Work magic on the dishes with her charm
A square of knitted string no more, no less
Yet faithfully she works at my command
Content to wallow in the grease and grime
Of endless pots and dirty pans combined
A humble task is but this dishcloth's lot
Yet with all vigour is the work attacked
Then when all's done and all is cleared away
She hangs up drying till another day.

Edith Hardman

SPEAK TO ME AS LOVERS SPEAK

Speak to me as lovers speak,
Say you've missed me for a while.
Say you've missed me for a week,
Or even for a day,
Speak to me as lovers may.

I've missed you I'd have to say,
More than a week, more than a day,
More than a year on bygone year,
Waiting for you to reappear.

So speak to me as lovers do,
Say you really have to go,
But you will stay if I want you to.
Speak to me in lovers' tones,
Shake me up and move my bones.

Speak to me in lovers sighs,
And take me by surprise.
Let us look into each other's eyes
And realise,
And realise.

Stewart Gordon

CONFLICT AND HOPE

From the hills that I used to walk
Comes the spittle of the dragon
Huge fireballs of destruction
Raining down on our homes

The dragon's children join their mother
They stutter out smaller, but just as deadly bolts of fire
These sprays of death cut down everything before them

The more experiences predators lurking in the bushes
Select their prey with the eyes of an eagle
With deadly accuracy their venom strikes
The victims unaware until it is too late

The dogs of war run down our hills
They destroy everything in their path
When all is quiet, the scavengers loot our homes
They take what they want, then return to their lairs

The evil master of these animals
Sits on his throne shouting out his orders
He savours the destruction he has caused
His appetite for this kind of meal is insatiable

From out of the clouds come a band of warriors
Their shields glistening in the sun
With their missiles they seek out the animals' larders
In the hope to destroy their supplies

As the warriors strike their targets
We on the ground see a ray of hope
But it is short-lived, the war dogs hit back
They have become more ravenous

We can only pray that eventually
When the war dogs are beaten into submission
We will be able to return to our homes
And like the phoenix rise and rebuild our land.

Jim Deehan

SEVEN JEWELS IN MY CROWN

Dear children of my children born,
Seven jewels in my crown.
Tom, the eldest, grown to manhood,
Husband, father of renown.

Heather, like a lily flower,
Lovely as the moon above,
Elegant and stately blooming,
Kind and gentle, filled with love.

Daniel – wandering through his childhood,
Turned the road and travelled far,
Soldier, hero, fighting terror,
Filled with joy and pride we are.

Oliver, approaching manhood,
At the gate of life you stand,
Calm, composed and sensible,
Success be yours on every hand.

Jesseca – a child of beauty,
Shining like a morning star,
Dancer, scholar, world's your oyster,
Strive, succeeding, going far.

Lovely Abigail, serene and
Tranquil as a summer sky,
What delights await your growing
Slowly, softly, by and by.

Chloe Ann, my youngest treasure,
Merry, pretty, laughing clown,
These children of my children born
Seven jewels in my crown.

Ann Dempsey

WATCHING OVER

The curtains were twain asunder,
Displaced by a gentle breeze;
Which enabled a shaft of moonlight –
To cast your silhouette against the wall;
Which, as I watched over spell-bound, –
Undulated with graceful ease;
And your porcelain-like skin in the pale purple light –
Was the purest ever seen.

I gazed on entranced as you lay serene;
The stress-lines of life lost forever in your dreams;
And your hair cascaded around you –
Glazed shimmery by the bouncing moonbeams.

I longed to hold you but held back,
As I watched over in silence, unseen;
Mindful that this magical moment in time would be gone,
For the dawn was soon to intervene.

Roger Oldfield

SWAN

Duke cob swan in robe of snow-white plume sat upon regal lake.
How the other British wildlife in great worship
And adoration of your mighty aristocratic being bow down,
To your leading, caring, heraldic wing flapping uprise
Stretching Heavenward upon the Serpentine.
A dream of King Arthur of this your Albion kingdom to be,
Festooned by the Westminster Cathedral audience, waves of loving bulrush,
Fanfared with royal waterlily triumphant fanfare,
Strewn in a pink confetti blossom,
Heralding you as the forthcoming sovereign of this Camelot realm,
Whence you, in matrimony, pass on by leaving
A high and mighty Blighty appreciative wake.
Companioned with Duchess that brings a majestic and elegant presence,
A future pen Queen Guinevere,
Together oakley entwined in a swan neck love heart that is, now married,
So lovingly sublime and gives to the world an assurance of the
Continuance of the royal fluttering standard and blue-blooded line.

Keith Newing

76

WET CAT, HARRY

I have no poem for Harry
His was a bitter case
Mine's a light and mild
Here's to Whiskey in your face
And if it's wet – please not water
A jug or two of ale
Reverse to story of Harry
His poem is this one well
Well, enough to water
Water is the word
Harry is our cat
And in his mouth a bird
Well, we fetch and carry water
To splash on Harry so
But Harry hung onto Bird
He would not let Birdie go
Well, Bird I think he's gone
To where dead birdies go
But Harry got a soaking
Wet Cat Harry, don't ya know.

Robert John Collins

LIFE AFTER RETIREMENT

You asked me, 'When I retire what do I do?'
I replied, 'You can do whatever suits you.'
You make whatever you want of your life,
A full-time mum, grandma and of course a wife
Look forward to the years that lie ahead
No more work, relaxation instead

When you retire life doesn't end
Take time with family visit a friend
Go shopping, the seaside, or the countryside
Retirement opens your world up wide
So enjoy your new life, you will be just fine
And on Monday morning you can say, 'My life is all mine.'

Patricia Maynard

QUESTIONS

Is it fluoride in the water?
Or the fingers getting tauter
Using waxed floss never should rush?
Correct use of special toothbrush?

Maybe visits to the dentist
Add those woodpoints to the long list
And no sugar should be tasted
So the time has not been wasted.

To keep our teeth from holes and stain,
Prevent the feel from any pain
To keep our gums conditioned pink
And breath so sweet, just stop to think.

Bright smiles to see and fresh it feels
The gateway to the body deals
To keep our teeth can then be seen
Perfection in good mouth hygiene.

Nina Jarman

WILD GENERATION

Here comes the generation
Where no one believes, no one cares
Dirt in the houses, garbage on the streets.
Full time leisure, be it disco or parties for pleasure.

Days, weeks and months fly away,
Yet we are laid back,
No more customs, no more tradition
What we call this is modern generation

As we look back,
We reflect on the memories
Biding us together with several ties,
Those golden days will last forever.

This is fact, this is the reality
We are lost in the generation era
No ways, no routes, no aid
We need to combat this raid.

Asma Osman Sattar

IN A COUNTRY CHURCH

As we drove to Devon on a hot summer's day
I noticed a church, half hidden away.
As I opened the door, I gave a gasp of surprise!
The church was decked with flowers for a bride.

Roses and lilies scented the air
Trailing green vines, arranged with care.
Wild flower posies at the end of each pew
Candles tall, waiting to glow.

'May you be happy, may your love never fail'
'As you stand, unknown couple, at God's altar rail'

Leaving the chancel, I discovered a stair
Which led to a chapel, for quiet thoughts and prayer.
Before Mary's statue, I knelt to say:
'Holy Mother teach me to pray.'

'Wake up sleepyhead,' said a voice in my ear.
'You have been fast asleep and we are nearly there.'
'Look the red cliffs of Devon and wide sparkling sea.'
'We will just be in time, for a delicious cream tea.'

Long years have passed since that holiday
And the dream I had on the way.
There is time now for quiet thoughts, and to say:
'Holy Mother, help me to pray.'

Meryl

POEM FOR THE WEDDING

A little girl sat on a creepy stool
In a cosy inglenook.
In the firelight's glow she looked pleased and content
As she held an open book.

And what did she see
As she sat there smiling?
Wonder of wonders
And magic, beguiling.

Yes, there's the castle
Very old
Very grand
Set in a beautiful wonderland.

There were turrets so high
That seemed to reach for the sky
And a drawbridge over the moat
And a gentle dove, the symbol of love
From the very prettiest dovecote.

There were deer to be seen
In woods so green
And a coach that was made of glass
And a prince with sword and scarlet coat
Enchanting to any young lass

And there's a princess in a glittering gown
All silver, gold and white
She looks so sweet, so the picture's complete
For the little girl reading that night

Many things have changed
Not a coach but a car
No swords or velvet cloak
But love never changes in warm-hearted folk

So it's true what they say
Fairy stories end the same way
They live happily ever after
We pray that this day
Will bring joy, love and laughter.

Stella Shepherd

SUILVEN

Viewed
from the icy fjords of The Minch
by Vikings marauding down the coast,
its seaward profile is a column of rock.
Its name in Norse
is Pillar Mountain.

Viewed
from the metropolis of Lochinver,
across the sea loch
and beyond Glencanisp Forest,
it is magnificent, improbable,
a dour, surrealistic, snow-besprinkled
but unsweetened Sugar Loaf,
a policeman's helmet carved in stone.

Viewed
from the north or south,
across peat bogs and lochan-strewn wilderness,
it is a recumbent pachyderm,
a slumbering mammoth with a noticeable waist,
lolling apart
from its siblings in the herd:
Canisp, Quinag, Cul Mor, Stac Pollaidh and Cul Beag.
Of all of these
it is the greatest and most magnificent.

And yet, surprisingly,
for all its fearsomeness,
Suilven's summit is benign:
viewed
from the cairn,
a field of gently-sloping grass,
a football pitch,
besprinkled with heather and clusters of edelweiss.

Norman Bissett

THE GOOD OLD DAYS

People called them the good old days,
There seemed so much in every way.
Out before nine, home by ten,
Or, 'You're not out this week again?'

We would simply say, 'Ah Mum'
Mum would always succumb.
It was as though the days went on forever,
The sun shone through whatever the weather.

Bottom of the garden stood the loo,
Newspaper cut, ready to use.
Always a visit before bed,
Mind how you go though! Mind your head!

Ration books, not so bad
Depended on what friends you had.
We always managed to eat,
Decent shoes on our feet.

Somehow we never wanted as much,
Well, never showed as such.
Waspy belt, tight skirts,
Fun to have that silly flirt.

Hard to remember when it was tough,
Good times, then rough.
Then Friday came, out we went,
Dancing, laughing – great moments spent.

Home before midnight,
Oh yes, alone.
Boys left behind.
Never brought home.

Sort out the handbag,
Smelly cig ends.
Well! Come on!
It was the trend.

So to another week
Work passing the ways,
Always to remember.
The good old days.

Margaret Elliot Woods

IF ONLY . . .

If only you could stay a while
So we could share some dreams
If we could only share a smile
But life's mapped out it seems
You had to go and leave me
You couldn't stay; you said
I know I haven't lost you
You've just gone on ahead

We'll meet again down Memory Lane
We'll tarry there a while
We'll dream our dreams
We'll share that smile
And you'll be home again
I'll find you when our time has come
At Heaven's gate we'll meet
Our life's full circle will be done:
Forever . . . Together . . . Complete.

Sheila Banks

BORN TO BE HURT

The chink of ice on glass
A low buzz of conversation
Abruptly silenced
All eyes transfixed

Nothing, nobody could live up to that
Is there any substance
Or just seven layers deep
Scant protection against the species

Now surrounding, encircling
Pain the specialty of the day
Innocence never sees until too late
The hurt suffered alone

So many yet so little conscience
The gene pool spread wide
All the bases covered
Beauty has no hiding place.

John Marshall

THE FIRST VINTAGE

Zeus, lord of light and god supreme,
Was startled by a vivid dream
Of fruits some purple, some light green
And all with bloom of velvet sheen.

He saw the bubbled clusters grow,
Ripening in intensive glow,
And with his powerful X-ray eyes
He watched the wondrous juices rise.

When Helios rose to bring the day,
Zeus called his wayward son from play,
For Dionysus had revelled in
The kind of pleasure we call sin.

He told his wanton progeny
That life was more than just a spree.
He must control his urge to frolic
And tend to matters more bucolic.

'Find ways of harvesting the juice
From all these grapes,' said mighty Zeus.
'Make of it a grand libation
Fit for the gods – a dedication.'

So Dionysus left his lord,
Quite chastened now and over-awed.
From purple grapes he drank the juice
Which stained his sensual lips bright puce.

With hoots of joy and loud hurrahs
He gathered vines in amphoras,
Then danced on them until they burst,
Making this vintage the very first.

With inspiration from Heaven sent
He let the glorious sap ferment.
He'd found the formula for wine
And christened it 'the drink divine'.

Celia G Thomas

UNTITLED

Little do you know
Of the reptile families
Freaked out by your wedding.
Baby birds will die
On your birthday,
Fox cubs panic
Just off
From your picnic.
Foul mouthed inconsiderate
Churns up the wood
For race track,
Destroys
In microcosmic reflection,
Fuelled by thrill
And sparks that bind.
Spiders scuttle
When you wake,
Rodents quake
And tiny mammals
Become instantly infertile.
Your howling blunderings
Of drunken Nazi
On nature trail,
Cause bugs
To fall on their swords.
The clouds gather,
The oxygen disappears,
And eternal sunset
Spreads beyond the horizon.
It was you
Who killed Cock Robin.

Paul Schofield

RAIN

It was lashing down the other day,
When I heard a friend of mine say,
'Isn't this awful – I wish it would stop,
What a terrible day'
Everyone in the group agreed,
Except one solitary man
'You're lucky,' he said, 'for where I come from,
You pray for it when you can.

You British don't know how lucky,
You really, truly are,
With your beautiful country – fertile land,
And seasons spaced out far,
Where I come from there is no grass,
Just sand and dusty soil,
Where we scratch to make a garden,
To grow veg – but it's vain toil.

For as soon as the wind begins to blow,
Our garden is blown away,
Because of water shortage,
We can't water every day,
You in this land just turn on a tap,
And pure clean water flows,
But in lots of other countries,
The water – it soon goes.

There are only certain times of day,
When water can be used,
And then it is rationed carefully,
In spite of people's views,
You can always put more clothes on,
To help you to keep warm,
But when the sun shines constantly,
It causes lots of harm.

Arid pasture – starving children,
Flies and plagues galore,
People dying from the measles,
Every year there's more,
So please don't take for granted,
This really lovely land,
For with all the rain – wind and snow
I tell you – it's real grand.'

Now after listening carefully,
To what he had to say,
I ventured out into the rain,
And blessed that lovely day,
For he's right about we people,
Our blessings we dismiss,
This land so green and fertile,
Is a truly precious gift.

I can't say I won't moan again,
When rain begins to fall,
But I'll spare a thought for those without,
And pray we don't get it all.

Dot Young

THE LONG ROAD

The road was long, it seemed never-ending.
And, as roads are, it was hard, and unbending,
My feet were sore.
And I was tired, but I had to carry on,
For there was more to be had,
In the place where I was headed
Arriving there, I knew I dreaded,
But I was told I had to be there,
Something awaited for me to share,
What that something was,
I did not know.
Really I did not care.
Would it be good? Or would it be bad?
What could it be?
Why had they sent for me?
What was this thing?
What could it mean?
Who would be there to share with me?
The further I walked, the less I felt,
That I should answer this strange summons.
But, it intrigued me, this mystery,
So, on and on, I plodded.

Grace Maycock

HAPPY TO SHARE MY THOUGHTS

Spiders everywhere explode into all directions,
Across the night-time sky of daytime.

Ever since God cast His spell,
By turning the world He created,
Onto its head, the wrong way up,
Just like a giant glass paper weight,
Showing a Christmas scene from winter.

So all the very things in life,
That we are all so passionate about,
Will unfortunately never last forever, now I'm certain.

Things like crimson sunsets,
Or winter wonderlands,
Where crystal-shaped snowflakes fall
But unfortunately, not forever, now will they last forever.

Or even also the fragile flight of
Bright and beautifully coloured butterflies,
Will also never last forever, somehow I'm certain.

But while such things of wonder and beauty do,
And all things on this Earth within this world flourish,
I will continue to look upon and at
All this world's very creations, for sure I'm certain.

Until my eyes close shut,
And I take my last breath of air into my lungs,
I will continue to enjoy all of
What someone or something has created.

Peter Walker

TEENAGE SON

Teenage son I love you so,
Can't you see that? Don't you know?
Strange creature to me, so hard to understand,
The way you act and try to command.
A clash of the Titans and butting of heads,
Treading on eggshells, watching what's said.
Like living with a time bomb waiting to explode,
Everything calm then *bang!* It's teenage mode.

I try to be patient and give motivation,
But you turn so quickly into Jekyll's creation.
I would love to chat like we used to,
I really miss that, do you?
Now the only time we converse,
Is when you want the contents of my purse.

You've the temperament of a wild stallion,
The attitude of Mr Medallion.
Mess and rubbish wherever you've been,
Do you even know how to clean?
You can be sweet and you can be funny,
It's usually part of a plan to get money.
You could sleep for England, you would win a medal by far,
At least while you are asleep I know where you are.

When I leave the house that's your cue,
To bring five or six others in just like you!
You eat all the crisps and drink all the juice,
Leave all the glasses then depart with an excuse.

But teenage son I love you,
I would have you no other way,
Your smile lights up a room,
To spend time with you makes my day.
I know you think I am an alien, on Earth as just a guest,
But I have lived the teenage years, so I think that I know best.

So let me tell you I believe in you,
And all the things that you can do,
When your raging hormones subside,
Our personalities will no longer collide.
When your temperamental metamorphosis is done,
You'll appreciate your ever loving, non-judgmental, ever caring mum.
Because I know who you are and I know you can,
Emerge a very lovely man.

Juliet Bence

BOY RACER

I turn heads.
You can hear me coming,
I make myself known
My key swaggers in the ignition
As I bounce down the road.

I turn heads.
No need for brakes, I'm a racer, mate.
Red means stop but I can't wait,
My rims keep rolling
I ain't got no time to waste.

I turn heads.
My bass shakes your bones.
I'm the engine revver,
The preposition shedder.
One hand's on the wheel the other's on my phone.

I turn heads.
Some call me reckless
But they're just jealous
Of my blinging necklace.
Too ready to correct the double negative.

I turn heads.
My engine's up your arse, in your grill
I'm on your tail mate
Speed is my thrill.
Doesn't matter what you do
I'm gonna overtake.

Keep up with the pace Grandad
I've got the bling, the boom, the va va voom,
Feel my rage, just listen to my ride
L plates get outta my face, before I swipe your side.

Foot on the accelerator, wearing my shades,
Cut the corner, crank up the bass, time to overtake.
Bus coming the other way, I'm out of my lane
No time to move over.

I'm turning heads,
Out of control, on a roll, if I stop, it'll be a miracle.
Brakes screech, glass shatters, I'm in a ditch
And the bus is in tatters.
I severed heads,
No bodies
Just bits
And roadside writs.

Beth Cortese

KNITTING

Cast on two stitches –
These are your parents.
Increase one more stitch –
This is the day of your birth.

Decide on a pattern –
Will it be plain knit and purl?
Perhaps you'll knit in some colours –
To make it more interesting?
It's looking good.

Ah, there are ten more stitches on the needle,
I see you have lots of friends,
The piece has grown longer.

What's happening now?
You've dropped some stitches.
Oh I see, you've lost old friends
– I am sorry.

You've lost the pattern
Have you run out of coloured wool?
Why are you casting off?
Oh, are you feeling tired?
Was it taking too long?

I see you're down to one last stitch –
Hang on in there, don't drop –
Off the needle!

Sally Dalby

THE DAY OUR QUEEN CAME DOWN OUR STREET

Over sixty years ago
Our princess became our Queen
My town put on a huge parade
The best you've ever seen
Mam made sure my Sunday frock
Was pressed and clean and neat
Then we stood in great excitement
As the parade came down our street
First we heard the horses' hooves
Clatter on the cobbled stone
And then the Queen came into view
Resplendent on her throne
She wore a cloak of crimson red
A dress of purest white
A golden crown upon her head
It was such a lovely sight,
I couldn't help but notice
Though I didn't cause a fuss
That she bore a strong resemblance
To the girl next door to us
The brass band played
'God Save the Queen'
Then the mayor, all hale and hearty
Announced that we were all to come
To a wonderful street party
With sandwiches and sticky buns
Sherry trifle and pork pies
Tables groaning with the weight
A feast for hungry eyes.
That night as I lay in my bed
The gastronomic treat
Was all that I could dream about
When the Queen came down our street
A child no more, at last I know
The Queen didn't come down our street
Her cloak was just a curtain
And her dress was just a sheet
The crown was just a scrap of card
Her carriage an old rag cart

But I hold on to the memory
And keep a place within my heart
For a very special lady
Who became our Queen that day
May God bless and keep her safe
And guide her on her way.

Christine Marley

ALONE

You wake in the morning, no one's there,
No one to talk to, no one to care.
The day stretches endless, nothing to do,
No one to care for, no one needing you,
Life is empty, all love is gone,
What is the use of carrying on?

People around you, but you are alone,
Locked in a world that's just one long moan,
Friends rally round you trying to help,
But all you can think of is yourself.

Why did you leave me? Why did you go?
No one can answer, no one knows,
But life must go on everyone says,
It will be better one of these days.
So you keep hanging on for a better way
You know it will come, but it's such a long day.

Joann Littlehales

WARNING

We can be sure another man will die
and that the dogs of war will find a way
to talk of glory as the drums beat out,
to talk of honour as the bugles sound;
and – should they stand and bow their heads – to say
it is for Queen and country, for the cause.

But other voices must be heard because
they intercede for souls assigned to die,
they tell of anguish and of grief, they say
in whispered words there is another way,
to save doomed youth from death and from the sound
of fury when the cannon thunders out.

Immortal poets, rise again, cry out,
urge Mammon to espouse a different cause
as battle cries across the land resound,
tell soldiers they were never meant to die,
the hapless sons of strangers, blown away,
brave mouthless men with nothing left to say.

Listen, my child, to what the generals say,
ask them what vague old lies they speak about
and ask them, too, to justify the way
they vaunt some spurious patriotic cause
before decreeing if you live or die,
with platitudes, with arguments unsound.

Listen, old man, the guns of Hell will sound
again today, no matter what you say,
their call to arms will mean more men will die,
will mean more body bags are counted out,
more priests employed, more eulogies to cause
more pain, more poppies strewn along the way.

Listen, you kings and princes, to the way
the poet speaks, be conscious of the sound,
the 'turbid ebb and flow' of lives that cause
battalions of learned tongues to say
the dogs of war are wrong, as men blot out
their dread forever 'up the line' to die.

Go on your way, good poet, now and say
no more. As trumpets sound, young men march out –
and do not know the cause for which they die.

Peter Davies

THE POTATO FIELD 1937

There's pocket money to be made
If only I can make the grade
Just plant the taters in the grooves
Cut by the plough and Bessie's hooves

A bucket of potato seed
Hard iron starts my leg to bleed
I place the tubers in the row
Now earth and rain will make them grow

I gaze upon the endless line
The sun burns hot, forever fine
Grandfather draws his hoe so quick
Thin arms that never miss a trick

Reflective, tired, once he said
Potatoes simply fill the shed
But we must toil our food to grow
God give us strength to make it so

August came fair with time to gaze
Long lines of green potato ways
With white and yellow blooms on top
Wait and hope for a heavy crop

September, brings the digging band
Our potato harvest, all by hand
In sacks, are barrowed and stored away
The field looks bare, autumn hold sway

Winter arrives, time spreading muck
When all is grey and damp and yuck
Now for some rest, us boys must sleep
To help the men to sow and reap.

Denis Pentlow

THE FIVE RINGS

The Olympics are upon us
So let's all celebrate
July twenty-seventh
Let's make it a date.
The world will arrive
In their colours so bold
In search of bronze and silver
And the elusive gold.

Years of meticulous preparation
In their quest to succeed
It's the Olympics after all
What more motivation do they need.
From all corners of the globe
They come in search of glory
Determined to do their best
And go down in history.

The five rings are the pinnacle
Of an Olympiad's career
To hear their national anthem
Will make them shed a tear.
But, of course, it's not just the winning
It's the feeling deep inside
To be there, London 2012
Wearing their colours with pride.

Robin Grigsby

THE SCENT OF LOVE

The hounds of Heaven
Pursue the scent of love.
Their baying echoes
In the forest of the night,
And the trees are alive
With the heady sap
Of desire,
As the hounds of Heaven
Pursue the scent of love
In the forest of the night.

Josephine Thomas

LYCRA BIKER

My name is Milton
From downtown Brixton
I'm on da dole
But I still got soul,
Cos I'm a Lycra biker,
I got plenty of style
I'm a serious cycler
I race every mile

Got aviator shades
Helmeted head
Snarl on me face
Jus' like Judge Dredd
Me head is down
Me legs are pumping
Doin' thirty an hour
And me heart is jumping

Me Spandex outfit's
Tight as skin
Shows me pecs
Holds me in
Wearin' Arsenal red
And Chelsea blue
I'm a kingfisher flash
From Electric Avenue.

Me Claude Butler frame's
Got a mean gear set
I can eat up de hills
Shed no sweat
I'm de king of da road
I'm da lord of de lanes
I don't care if it shines or rains.

I'm sleek, I'm a streak
I'm in peak form
I got pride, I like to ride
In de eye of da storm.
Yeah, I got no job
But I'm no reject
Man, when I'm on two wheels
I got self respect.

Antony Matthews

PACEMAKER

My day dawns
Yawns
Sleep of the just
Just before
Surgery
Has been perjury
Now nurses
No curses
Nothing but smiles
And service
One particular nurse
Treasure
Get on well together
Nil by mouth
Windows looks south
Delightful morning
Final yawning
Sip of water
Here comes porter
Come along sir
Stir
Heart scan
Still working
Now and then jerking
Soon to be sorted
To theatre transported
Camera focal
Anesthetic local
Pacemaker inserted
Heart alerted
All time awake
Shoulder will ache
Don't use arm
Cause harm
Back to ward
Same delectable nurse
Secretly I curse
If I were fifty years younger!

Ronald Jameson

THE WAR CORRESPONDENT

This may be the last time
That we say goodbye
This may be the last time
That you catch my eye.
This may be the last time
That I feel your tender kiss
Of all the things in life
That's the one thing I would miss.

This may be the last time
You tell me to take care
This may be the last time
Our devotion we can share
This may be the last time
I see your smiling face
Please wish me the best of luck
While I'm in that war torn place.

This may be the last time
That I see the land I love
This may be the last time
I need help from up above.
This may be the last time
My reports are in the news
I know about the dangers
But it is the life I choose.

David Corkill

HERE WE GO

Poetry readings
Very popular in Derbyshire
Indeed
This year's 'Poetry With Punch'
A sell out.
I cannot claim anything like that.
I have read to the WI
The U3A.
OAPs
Disabled clubs
Primary school children
Fellow poets at festivals I have organised
Made people cry
Made people laugh
Been published
Been rejected
Too many times
So forget the Arkwright Rap.

David Robinson

MINE

Once there were so many of them
Scarring the face of my green and pleasant land
With wagon-ways, the acne of pit heaps
Mineheads, all the paraphernalia of power
Needed to power Stephenson's locomotives
Then Swan Hunter's steamships
While deep underground men and children
Toiled like human moles for the black gold.

But where are they all now?
Vanished like the mist on a summer's morn
As though they had never been born
While the constant unchanging features remain
The gently rolling hills patchworked with purple moors
Looking down to the golden singing sands by the cold North Sea
The wine-sweet air, the chattering streams
But best of all, the border folk
Sturdy and steadfast and cheerful
People of my heart and dreams.

Meg Gilholm

LETTER TO HEAVEN

I know you're not hard to reach
You're just a prayer away
But it gets harder and harder
To not see you every day

So I'm writing you this letter
To know that we're okay
If you ever need to reach us
We're never far away

It would be nice to hear from you
Even though it must be hard
I miss your eyes and smile
Even writing your birthday cards

I know one day we'll meet again
Even though I'll have to wait
In many years I'll see your face
And you'll see me at Heaven's gate

The stars are brighter and
When I look up I shed a little tear
Because I always remember
That you're not here

I wish Heaven had a phone
Because I'd call you every day
Just to check up on you
And make sure you're not alone

I hope God gets this letter
And passes you my love
Then you'd have a part of me
Until the clouds I am above

I'm sending God this letter now
I can't wait to see you again
I love you with all of my heart
My dear friend.

Jennifer Howell

THE PASSENGER

Intriguing, the face across the aisle
A slightly nervous look and though I mustn't stare, a head of pale and whispy hair and just the
ghost of a smile
Someone to study as I sit and try to read a rather tedious file
And somehow stifle the boredom as the train lurches by – mile upon tedious mile
Yet I seem compelled to stare into the gloomy sky and give up on my book and put away my file
And consider how the brave plants bloom along the ragged track,
And wonder that they live at all, despite the care they lack
When I see them grow abundantly between abandoned rails
And leave some telling trails of ferny green
As, inconsequentially, I dream
I must return again,
To investigate, subtly of course the passenger on the train
Her dress is unmemorable, unfashionable and black and yet she isn't old
And then between her slender fingers a newspaper unfolds
I strain to read the headlines, they appear to be quite wrong
The paper seems quite yellow and yet the lights are strong
I see a date below the heavy black and bold strapline
I double check the figures which spell nineteen thirty-nine
These headlines are the stories from a bleak and distant time
This must be for her research or theatrical design
I think I'll pose a question, with some quickly thought-up line
But suddenly the seat is free, I turn and shift position
I see her vanish seamlessly through the train's partition
 I know beyond all doubt and sense, I've seen an apparition
By now the passengers have left, departed from the train
It's happened very quickly and I'm left here on my own
I feel quite peaceful sitting here, and yet I must go home
And then I see the platform and I'm beckoned to come down
'You've reached your destination,' says the man who called my name
The train has left without me and the journey starts again
The passengers had been talking in hushes and muted tones
'I thought he was asleep,' one said, 'although he gave a gentle moan
And then the file slid to the floor and the book that he had read
It happened very suddenly, life is a tenuous thread'
'They've come to take him from the train,' said the lady dressed in black
'I'll pick some flowers for him that grow beside the ragged track'
Then she drifted seamlessly through the solid station fence
And never once looked back.

Margaret Whitehead

THE SILVER BIRDS
(Commemorating Battle of Britain)

Their world, full of the high ideals that took them to the skies . . .
With diffident, courageous grace they sped away . . . from youth . . . now to
Determined men, the light of battle in their eyes . . .
Their world, uncertain and so darkly real, yet as a dream in trust
Upon the expectations of mankind, thinking only of what lie ahead,
Maybe a prayer, to meet the challenge that was theirs to find . . .
A hellish view instinct had to guide, a battlefield upheld by metal
Power . . . in all the world there was no place to hide, full face on,
Conscious only of the moment . . . no time for fear to show its face in such a death defying race .
. . Braver than their hero hearts would ever say . . . just another masquerade, another day . . .

Who came back, was what mattered most, when splintered bone and metal side by side was
scattered on an easy ribald boast, twisted by a conflict that had lied . . . Friendship was mutual
brotherhood, defying
Time, aware of the full cost, failing to return one by one,
The lights dimmed for everyone who lost . . . but in the name of those who went before,
It became the thing to try and even up the score . . .
Yet despite it all,
Somehow, they wore Death, a girdle of distain, contemptuous, because they really knew,
Time could be just a borrowed hope - it was always now . . . you . . . or . . . them.

It was a courage unsurpassed by time,
A challenge unforsaken in release,
A symbol of a century's design,
A world, still searching for a way to
Lasting peace . . .

Colleen Biggins

THE CRYSTAL GAZER

The crystal seemed heavy to hold as it drew my gaze,
Then I seemed to be gazing into a luminous sphere,
A vast ethereal globe all moving light,
With fleeting flashes of rainbow beautiful flame.
I watched its strange opalescence, and changing lights,
Entranced. Then lo it cleared, and it seemed I saw
In its centre our sun with his planets burning enringed,
But no longer a central sphere of intrinsic gold,
But a spheric omnipresence, a mighty being
Embracing the whole of the solar manifest,
Wherein moved the planet fires. I gazed as a seer
Daring the holy secrets inviolable;
Here was the source and centre, the soul and spirit,
The range and circumference of Man's universe,
Here, and within my vision, within my grasp,
Exultant my expanding spirit within me leapt,
And then 'twas gone – and lo, in my hands a ball,
A clairvoyant's crystal, I gazed at it marvelling.

Henry Harding Rogers

THE PASSING OF THE ROCK GENERATION

Hard on the heels of youth rides middle-age,
Rough-shod, trampling tender dreams, snorting contempt,
And then the twilight years with stiffened fingers turn the page,
Bald pate shining, grisly beard unkempt,
Yet eager to prove the drama still runs apace
And dreams, though lying fallow still,
Might yet bear fruit, not have to face
The awakening of death. No, no, the kill
Has yet to come, my naïve baby-boomers,
Kaftan-clad, trailing clouds of pot.
Forget the rumours of Nirvana and embrace your fate.
Immortals we are not and cannot legislate
Eternal youth. For we shall soon be gone before
As sure as all the rest.
You'll feel the rocking drumbeat hesitate inside your chest
And off to oblivion you'll be gone
With peace and love and ban the bomb.

David J Ayres

104

FOOD FOR THOUGHT

Have you ever given thought to your fellow human's lot?
not all humans are the same we differ in many ways
language plays a part in this, in culture, history and religion
plays a part in moulding us and where we fit in all of this
mankind has come a long long way from the dark ages
till today, progress made in many ways and wars that
played a part in this

But human beings will always fight, for what they believe is
right and most wrongs are put to right, and we make
another start, but not a lot has changed today there's
people who have no say in matters in the World
today a different race a different breed their fate
decided by human greed, extermination and
genocide

Terrorism plays its part in wrecking lives and breaking
hearts with young soldiers dying in foreign streets
fighting an enemy they can't see dying senselessly
a worthwhile cause some will agree, when sons and
daughters do not return and husbands leave
a family where can their loved ones turn

When I was six years old I experienced what like
it was to be terrified, in nineteen forty-one on
the thirteenth of March Clydebank my home
town was bombed to the ground by the Germans
only three homes were left standing many people
died in the two nights we were bombed

Do you sit back and say I'm alright I have three
meals a day a place to lay my head and clothes
on my back I wonder will you still sleep at night
after reading my poem.

Alexander H Grozier

SILVERADO AND PEARL

Hey, it didn't look likely
Cos money was tight
But we hooked up together
And it worked out alright
There was Turtle and Fish
With Pearl and then me
Away on the west coast
Where the surf roars wild and free
Out with the Silverado boys
And a pearl from the sea
The cool, cool Silverado boys
And Pearl, such a pear from the sea.

The guys came down from 'Cisco
Where the Bushman made them smile
When I flew in to Lindbergh Field
They'd been at the Cove for a while
And we stayed on there together
And bunked down in one room
'Longside Woolsey and Bob at Turtle's side
While gulls were screaming in the gloom

The pelicans swooped, the seals just stank
Grey skies closed in, the weather raged
We had to wait: we ate, we drank
Vanilla malts at the burger lounge, blueberry pancakes at the Cottage
There were spicy ribs and big bang shrimp
Hot tamales, eggs, burritos,
Delicious fish from El Pescador
Some quesadillas with chorizo
Laughing with the Silverado boys
And a pearl from the sea
Turtle and Fish Silverado
And Pearl, such a pearl from the sea.

From Scripps Pier down to Wipeout Beach
The choppy, crumbly waves increase
As the old guy's jaw, Fish scowlscans for swell today
But an onshore wind disintegrates the spume and spray
Little dude Turtle dives and splashes
His laugh caught in the wind-tossed
Rolling Pacific waters that surge and crash,
His sparkling body looks embossed with diamonds
Splashing with the Silverado boys
And a pearl from the sea

The glittering Silverado boys
And a rare lustrous pearl from the sea.

The mini mal, the booger,
The fishtailed short board's wrapped
We're headed down to Tourmaline
The set-up's waxed and strapped
Driving south along Coast Boulevard
The best tunes are blasting our way
And 94.9 says a swell's coming in
So there's gonna be surfing today
Riding waves with the Silverado boys
And a sweet precious pearl from the sea
The sun-bleached Silverado boys
And Pearl, such a pearl from the sea.

Pearl and Fish paddle, glossy-black,
Way out to hang for rides
As the old guys on their longboards, baseball-capped, track
The mellow rush of rippling tides
And closer still, where the splurge of waves cascade,
Little dude, on the booger, is the king of leap-shoot-glide
In boardies and Ramones T-shirt he wins hands down, each accolade
The high-fived smiles for most waves caught, the slickest slide
Watching there as the Silverado boys
And a smooth silken pearl surf the sea
The salty Silverado boys
And Pearl, such a pearl from the sea.

Above teams of stinging jellies,
Catfish, ray and more
The foam-flecked green-blue ocean
Beat a rhythm to the shore
As freckled and bedazzled,
Our time together flows
Slipping like sand-grained bubbles
Through our lashes, fingers and toes
And now we move in separate break
Glad of such an improbable collision
Shadow-dancing Californian days

In a soothing repetition,
Recalling La Jolla in the summer of '9
As our best tunes kept coming on 94.9
Pumpkins and Rancid, Weezer and Leon
This was the trip that I wanted to be on
Away with the Silverado boys
And a pearl from the sea.

Lauren Huxley-Blythe

FOR A DREAM LOST

Secret longing all my life
To be a mother and a wife

Wife came easily it seems, but motherhood remained in dreams

O cruel, cruel twist of fate
This body changing far too late

All the signs of new life stirring
Fills my heart, deep pangs of yearning

Knowing it can never be
Age has stolen youth from me

Tiny seed of hope within
Crushed as soon it begin

Examinations, ultra sound,
Emotion swirling round and round

Consultants, tests and CT scan, never part of natal plan
How? This abdomen distending as a pregnant womb thus gnaws
Breasts enlarging, aching, swelling, gripping heart with pincered claws

Curse oh curse the menopause.

Jennifer Densham

MONEY FOR AN OUTING

Bags pour through the door for charitable causes; diseases, children, old folk; asking for clothes, shoes, books, toys, CDs, DVDs and rags for people with flags of all nations.
Another grand sort out now what can I throw? Some T-shirt tops and my husband's old shirts and socks, as for old rags they can go into the bag the rest to one side they must bide for the local Girl Guides are having a jumble sale and what is more, I have been roped in to man a stall.
The day has arrived all bright and clear, luckily the church hall is quite near, I am first in it seems and up go the tables,
Bulging black sacks all need to be sorted, adults on this table, children's on that,
Oh good here come the mothers; the busy ones the docile ones and the far too intelligence ones with no realistic skills.
Nobody wants to man a bric-a-brac or clothing just the cake table, tombola or raffle,
And up goes a cackle of who wants to do what so they can sell up quickly and sit down with a cup of tea.
They are all interrupted by a terrific crash,
Some bric-a-brac has fallen, the table is laden.
Boxes of books have arrived, some old ones in there.
I hope they all sell or someone's husband will go spare for keeping them at home is a great 'bug bear'.
Bed linen to put out it takes up a great deal of room and will soon spread down to the toys; there is not enough room for the boys' clothes,
Those handbags and belts will just have to go into some boxes under the table and we can get them out when we are able.
The Girl Guides have 'done us proud' everyone agrees.
At last we are ready, now for a cup of tea before the door opens and they all stampede.
Here come the 'car-booters, the eBayers and the sellers' running, elbowing, grabbing, armfuls of clothes keeping us all on our toes for the ones who pilfer and secrete – it can be quite a feat.
They peer at the bottom of china with glee as if someone would part with antique pottery.
The jewellery too is carefully inspected for silver or gold or watches that are decidedly old and worth some money if it be told.
There is junk and there is treasure for all to buy and in fact anything that catches the eye.
Somebody has won a hamper and beer, some people are disappointed I fear.
Exhausted we clear up the rest of the things and someone is counting up the huge takings.
A most successful day has been had and really my feet aren't that bad!

Jenny Kain

AL'S SLIM-IN WISHING-WELL APPEAL

Our brother Alan decided to slim
And asked if we would all sponsor him
We all said of course
Because the money was for a good cause
There's Babs, Jean, Edna, Fay, Lucy and Pearl
Jane, Carol, Mary, Joe and Shirl
Then there's Andrew who's slim enough
When climbing stairs he doesn't puff
Alan's wife June is the one who said
You can have just one slice of bread
It's salad lunch, grilled fish for dinner
This is making our Alan slimmer
The fat it seems just melts away
He gets thinner by the day
He started this in mid-July
We all said, 'It's just a ploy'
He's tried before but couldn't keep
To any kind of diet sheet
When he whistled through clenched teeth
We all made a hasty retreat
Everyone knew he was feeling bad
This diet nearly drove him mad
As weeks went by, Alan was slimmer
We all noticed his waist was trimmer
He lost a stone and now he knows
What it feels like to see his toes
He told us that he would lose two
But he just couldn't see it through
Don't despair now Christmas is here
He'll be doing exactly the same next year.

James Gobbin

ON SEEING BATH

Upon a fine autumnal day
I gazed on Bath's fair face
The buildings rose about me
With dignity and grace.

The ancient abbey towering high
A symbol of Christian light
Looked down upon another place
A Roman bathing site.

I stood beneath an archway there
My thoughts began to stray
As in my mind a picture formed
Of a far-off Roman day.

Perhaps upon the waters side
A legate drank his wine
Whilst silently appraising
A sculptured form divine.

Or else in one dark corner
A plot was given life
Which helped to re-shape history
With the quick stroke of a knife.

I wandered on through thoroughfares
Where Georgian houses stand
And came upon another place
The assembly rooms so grand.

When Beau Nash graced the grand salon
In fashionable Georgian stance
A fortune might be lost or won
Upon a game of chance.

The time had come for me to leave
I did so with regret
For those few hours I spent in Bath
I never will forget.

Terence Iceton

SUNDAY AT A GOLF COURSE ON LONG ISLAND

DAYBREAK

The rain fell hard last night upon
This field of dawn where golfers play.
A harbinger invading a green land lost
To April floods and melting snow.
But now the sun lifts up into the middle of a clear – no –
Almost a clear sky. There, over there, clouds creep
Low-peering, lingering shadows, dying –

Random thoughts of which
The human being
Is not so capable.

MIDDAY

'Fore!' someone screams, and the white ball lifts
Up into the sky, hanging there for an instant as if a perfect sun
But reaching no higher than the dying trees
Below in the valley. Randomly it comes to rest near a ragged puddle
Overflow from the lake
During the night.

A light chuckle from the players, as
Tight-pressed and clean, they struggle along
To the next tee, dressed in happy colours and
White soiled shoes with matching gloves
To protect their hands. Hats, umbrellas too – all create
A gentle motley stained by the sun into a single silver hue.
The players' eyes laugh, bright still

With whisky of the night before, sipped with oh! Such
Ease! Such elegance! Such terror.
But now the sun shines gently above
And beyond their forlorn silhouettes
Forming foolish question-marks to the sky
Struggling gamely like dying animals
To the next tee
Near the black puddle.

AFTERNOON

Look, can you see it?
In the puddle by the lake, nearer the wildflowers –
Wrapped in broken grass and mud –
It is a fish – no – he is a trout.

112

With spring air sparkling in laughter on his cool smooth skin
And sunlight splashing roundly on his silver eye – look –
He's playing, he's dancing – no – he is struggling, he is dying.
The puddle narrowing like an eye in the heat
The killing sun sucking his dark life dry.
Unnoticed in the midst of this leisure green day, this happy light day.
He breathes heavily, rhythmically, sucking
The hot air into thin fragile gills
Lying on his side, waving glistening fins
Like a gentle bird's wing, back and
Forth, back and forth. The fin nearer
The water slaps it vacantly, the other
Waves into a sky so empty now, so random.
His eye so clear and dark and round!
Stares beyond the omnipresent puddle and the
Approaching players joking and laughing among themselves.

Silently waiting.
Watching. As death flows in
And around.

Joanne Weiss

TEARS RISING TO HEAVENS GRAND

As silver tears, roll upon the floating cloud, all burdens of the passing years, pass on yonder to Bula Land.

Where God enthroned, in splendorous glory, with all His angels in attendance stand.

He waits for the silver tears of His special child, He waits for them to gently fall away, whence He catches them in His hand.

The silver tears say, 'Catch me please, catch me, let us rest in Heaven along with the silver cloud.'

'We each have a story to tell, whispered to us by our earthly soul of life's burdens and woes and hopes lost, we have been shed in thousands.'

'But since our friend soul has been saved we too have become precious in Your sight.'

'Like silver, like gold, like diamonds, we silver tears now float close to Heaven upon a cotton wool cloud, no longer falling to dirty ground.'

'We know we rise, to be caught by Jesus Christ.'

He says, 'I know these tears and the fears beyond – come, I'll show you Heaven's grand.'

Barbara Fletcher

THE LEGEND OF LUFFENHAM HEATH
CHRISTMAS EVE 1911

I'll tell you a story, remember it well,
Of Luffenham Heath and young Gypsy Nell.
For she was a princess just barely sixteen
The daughter of Rachel, a Romany Queen.

Their Christmas encampment, this always had been
On Luffenham Heath where never was seen
A happier gathering of wayfaring folk
Singing at night by their bright campfire's smoke.

Now this year a wedding had been planned for young Nell
To Philip the tinker, a lad she loved well.
A home he had made her with wheels red and green
The prettiest caravan she'd ever seen.

From all over England their families had come
To Luffenham Heath to join in the fun,
But when they arrived at their old camping ground
They found it fenced off with wire all around.

Then up spoke Nell's father, 'Since ever I've known
It's been common land with freedom to roam,
To stop here we all have a God given right.'
So they tore down the fence to make camp for the night.

It's said that the Earl, with anger consumed
That his plans for a golf course might through them be doomed,
Commanded his bailiff to drive them away
And wanted it done by the end of the day.

That night by their campfire the welkin was ringing
With music and dancing and laughter and singing,
When up rode the bailiff with fifteen armed men
And ordered them off to be not seen again.

In vain they protested. Then violence broke out
And several gypsies were killed in the rout.
While Philip and Nell were both of them slain
Then the tribe were moved off in the sleet and the rain.

Their bodies were buried there on the Heath,
With nothing to mark them, not even a wreath.
And though people knew, no one dared say a thing
For fear of the wrath from the Earl it might bring.

Now golf is still played there, but some people say,
That the ghosts of the gypsies remain to this day,

For many an evening there's scarcely a sound
Where the ill-fated lovers lie still underground.

While every few years, as the seasons roll by
The grass where their camp stood will wither and die
And never is heard there, not even in spring,
A robin or thrush or the nightingale sing.

Januarius

LAND OF MY BIRTH

Let me wander over this land of my birth
To feel free and sense the wind blow its coldness
Stinging against the face
And to smell the sweet-scented heather on Nature's breath
Above a curlew's cries sound as he circles around
In space.

Onward I roam where the fallow deer gaze amid the
Forest's resplendent in their autumnal haze
The setting sun creating an aura over a backdrop to
Be framed
The beauty of this valley is all around to see as
I traverse far yonder a pleasurable sight greets me
Down through the rugged area a brook gurgles noisily
There rabbits scamper aimlessly in wild frivolity.

For miles I seemed to have travelled over this
Land that was my birth
Stopping for a moment taking in this wondrous scenery
The sweat and toil which had gone into fashioning
The rocky crags and glens
Are down to the industrious labour from its past
Hardworking men
Who had once walked over this land that had been their
Birth
Proud of one's heritage now lie buried within its earth.

Valerie Thompson

RIVER REFLECTIONS

Windswept sea pushed rough dirty waves,
Onto the shore and into the caves.

White puffed-up clouds in sky above blue,
Brightness of sunshine filleting through.

Yachts out there anchored to red floating buoys,
Blustering, tossed, like small childish toys.

Tide on the ebb, leaving flotsam on shore,
Mud slimy and slippery, jetsam and more.

Turn over the rocks to find winkles and crabs,
Or, if you are lucky, some tasty small dabs.

Children in wellies, mud up to their thighs,
Buckets and spades in their hands making black pies.

Tiny squeals of delight are heard all around,
Find a crab, when it nips, drop it back to the ground.

Windsurfers unpack their boards and their sails,
Today with this wind they won't go like snails.

View across river, farmhouse with green lands,
It all looks so small and quiet as it stands.

From over that side comes the ferry, quite slow,
Steered by sunburnt man they all call 'Joe'.

Watch now for the yachts, just starting their races,
Full billowing sails, men with spray on their faces.

This simple coastline on a warm summer night,
With so much to watch a true river sight.

It's very quiet now, not a person in view,
Just me with my thoughts and nothing to do.

But I think and I marvel of things made by God,
From sky to the Earth, Heaven and sod.

Look around and wonder at what you can see,
This Earth and this Heaven made for all, and for me.

Time seems to stand still, but not so the tide,
The moon is its mentor to obey and abide.

No way can we stop it, it never will cease,
So just sit and wonder and you will feel peace.

Red reflections on water, could it be Mars?
No, it's the sunset before moon and stars.

Try to hold on to this bright burning light,
But it's no good, it has gone! It is night!

But now that it's gone just darkness abounds,
Soft waters lapping the mud, murmuring sounds.

Time to go homewards and leave waters so deep,
And dream of tomorrow in God-given sleep.

Frances Pitt

ODE TO GRANDCHILDREN - MATTHEW AND EMILY

When family has family –
We rejoice the special day,
Not knowing of the heartache
That sometimes comes your way,
We do our very best for you –
Nothing is too much trouble,
But in this time that we now live,
We get problems by the double.
We give, we fetch, we carry –
We feed every Stephen, Greavesey and Harry,
But somehow this does not suffice,
Computers take the day –
Your mobile phones ring all the time
We cannot find a way
To make you see that Grandparents
Are not here just to be used,
And would sometimes like a
Please and Thank you
To be in the set of rules.

Judith M Cripsey

REMEMBERING

My happiest memories are when I was young
My family together forever having fun.

We played games in the evenings
Ludo, tiddlewinks and cards
We laughed all the time.
The closeness of our love and understanding
Stays with me, memories are mine.

Holidays were special, travelling by train
Arriving with the family, sandcastles to make
Swimming in the sea.
Playing with other children, lots of games on the beach
How happy, that was me.

Schooldays were special, my sports days were best
The worst being arithmetic and taking a test.

I never forget the ice cream van, the music was very loud
We all queued for our ice cream cornet
Frozen lollipops, my what a crowd.
Our grocery man came with his horse-drawn cart
Supplying everything from a pin to a tart.

The coalman came with his sacks full to the top
With his coal and nutty slack,
The trademan called at our door with lemonade
And dandelion and burdock in stone jars,
Empty ones to take back.

I need to relive my memories even more
No one can take away my youth,
Remember having ration books 'd's and 'e's
For sherbet fountains and liquorice
Even with a sweet tooth.

Playing hopscotch, spinning a top and skipping
All the things we did for fun
Scrumping and door knocking was naughty
My parents said should never be done.

My most vivid memories were at Christmas
We all took part in that.
Shopping Christmas Eve for our tree, a turkey
And my Dad's six and seven eights hat.

We cannot go back to that wonderful time
But can remember forever these memories of mine.

Joan Marrion

ONE EYE A-SHINE

Open the curtains as the sun reaches forth
And feel the warmth as if never before
Inhale the sweet scent of a flower so rare
And the sweetest of birdsong is carried alongside the air
Risen from the East this new day will dawn
A glimpse – caught the sight of a new breathing fawn

Through the meadow we venture far
As away does fall the final bright star
Through the water we tread so fine
Reflections will glisten – in one's eye a-shine
Through the pages of a story we continue to read
Creating the image – the one we so dream

In a field afar newborn lambs, so fluffy and white
As out from the burrow soft bunnies see first light
The robin's nest atop the tree, sits high and safe
Two butterflies together give the most colourful chase

From East rose the sun which gave birth to this beautiful day
Now to set softly, has this all been a dream?
As I close my eyes, do I open them again?
Will tomorrow be as vibrant as today?
Night's call begins to echo
From the West comes the richest orange glow
Down on the world from my cloud I look
A shine in my eye; this Spring I'll never forget.

Samuel Burgess

TURMOIL

A hurricane is predicted:
time, place – we aren't sure,
No time to stand and stare,
fear grips us, we panic, unsure
what we should do.
Try to keep calm.

When it impinges, where will we be?
On the bus, on the train, down by the sea?
Where is safety? Home might be –
No time to think, the seconds flash by.
Try to keep calm.

Will the sea defences hold?
The grey waves rise up and sink down
you can smell the salty spray.
Thoughts of survival, what is the best thing to do,
crowd my mind.
There is no time to ponder, quick decisions
are needed now.
Try to keep calm.

The sky darkens, suddenly the wind becomes
violent, the hurricane is insane, a raging storm,
it rips things apart, uproots trees,
tears down telegraph poles –
it's strong, forceful, so powerful.
This tempest is no respecter of persons.
It tries to take your breath away
is out of your control.
Try to keep calm.

The seagulls whirl overhead in confusion.
plastic bags fly and catch on tree branches.
When will it abate? No telling.
Everyone is weary.
Try to keep calm.

Mary Chalk

THREE TO ONE

'I can't go on.'
So many times the strain
Seems too much.

'I can't go on.'
The agony, that fearful pain
Seems like such –
'I can't go on.'

The aim of life is gone
And tired and wearied,
'I can't go on.'

Again and again in so much pain
The skilful surgeon's knife
Has barely saved my life
But because he's done his job –
I do mine, and fight to lob
Another smile again.

Each time it seems I sink beneath another wave,
I think I die; hurt as I am, the warming breath restores my ailing health – I try again.
The story goes that when I say
'I can't go on,' in Heaven I pray
And back the speedy answer comes,
'It's three to one, you won't succumb
Because on your side, close at hand
Power, love and sanity band –
To cast out fear.' For God does say, 'That fear is not
What holds life's sway
But confidence in my supreme power
To pass you through your painful hour.'
So it's three to one I can go on
To live the life I'm set upon;
The route is not what I would wish
But divine judgment hold the dish
To give me the nature He will spare
And through eternity will share
His power, His love and His peace of mind.

Sandy Brenda Chapman

CHRISTMAS

Go not, November, haste not so soon away,
The year is turning, day by day;
Prey spare us the relentless tread,
Of swift December. Enough said.

The iron fist of expectation
Hangs over Christmas celebration.
I'll tell you what it's all about,
The fear of leaving someone out.

Christmas, a time of much ado,
Cards, letters, parcels, presents too.
Each one to carry on its way,
A loving wish, cordiality.

Christmas is here – the deadlines beckon,
With more demand then you could reckon,
Why must it be the 25th,
Why not the 29th or 30th?

Sure 'tis the time of frantic quest
To gather in a goodly fest.
Decorations all about;
And radiant lights, inside and out.

The search for gifts that will augment
A good friend's interest, special bent.
Toys that will sure give satisfaction,
Not drive good parents to distraction.

Busy streets, drivers hard pressed
To stretch the last few days that's left.
I'll wrap my car in one thick rubber frame.
I wish each other driver'd do the same.
'Twould save my poor wee slave from scrape and score,
Just for one week 'ere Christmas, nothing more!

All is not lost, in spite of ills,
A precious sacred wine distills.
There is a feeling in the air,
Pervades the merry festive glare.

Great singing from ten thousand choirs,
Carols we all together sing.
Transcendent music that inspires
The timeless song that Christmas brings.

For Christmas comes Heaven's influence to express;
A kindly word and freedom to transgress

The normal stance of cautious reticence
Trysts with lone friends we haven't seen for ages,
For Christmas will brook no procrastination.

Black Santa's there the whole day long,
And folk who leave the busy throng,
To multiply the good saint's score,
And cherish Christmas all the more.

Friends and relations, songs and Christmas trees,
And children revelling in their fantasies
With shrill acclaim, and Christmas night well spent,
Responding to their merriment.
Drink! 'Tis the wine of human love,
So merry Christmas!
To our Lord, above.

Florence Lyster

THE GRATING SPEECH

I started orating
True story narrating
The facts I am stating.

The crowd aren't spectating,
Instead they're berating,
And my speech negating.

It is so frustrating,
Each sentence they're hating,
And giving a slating.

With confidence deflating,
My brain is now stagnating,
No more pontificating.

And now my heart's pulsating,
I think my head's rotating,
My body is gyrating.

Down through the grating
Grating
Grating . . .

Is this grating on you
Like it's grating on me?

Mary A Peace

YOU'RE BEING WATCHED

Little eyes are watching
Every single day
Watching all that you may do
Hearing what you say
They take in all the good things
But also all the bad
That which makes us happy
That which makes us sad

Little minds are working
Ticking round the clock
Taking note of what they hear
Whether good or not
Little ears are listening
To all which may be said
Forming opinions
In their tiny heads

How sad if what they see
Is far from being good
How sad if what they hear
They really never should
How sad if in their tiny minds
Opinions root and grow
Thoughts which they should never think
Or things they should not know

What children see
What children hear
What others do or say
From within a child's mind
Patterns day by day
Patterns to enhance their lives
Or patterns to destroy
So be careful what you say or do
With wisdom bring them joy.

Dorothy Durrant

HURRICANE LOVE

Your eternal love is like the dramatic entrance of a hurricane in all its glory
Crashing, banging, thumping and forcing itself into my heart with no worry
Knocking passionately at the core of my soul, daring to penetrate, to capture me
The wind of desire is so strong I can barely concentrate, breathless waiting to see
The whistling and cracking of trees of hope blowing debris of affections my way
Saturating the environment of my inner being as you strive to have your say

Inviting your invigorating presence assured that there isn't any defeat in you
The thunder and water soaks and nourishes me right through and through
The shutters of my heart open to let your fierce frenzy unconditional love in
Overwhelming spasms of yearning swells throughout and it is not a sin
Floods of seductive stares glisten and touch my body, soul and mind
As it overtakes respect gently trickles in the scenery and works to bind

The thunderous instrument of awakening passion clouds over every emotion
Lightning sparks that burning sensation shocking me into the right motion
Tasting the sweetness of the pure joys of your wondrous love which is mine
The ecstasy constantly poured at my door sending shivers down my spine
Challenging me with the powerful thrust of untold treasures and delights
Of oneness we can't measure, reaching avenues, taking us to untold heights

The tidal spray of happiness surging and embracing a grip of fantasy existence
Where the obvious become camouflaged in a web of caresses and intimacies
Oh mighty wind of tenderness wait patiently at my feet and let me taste
The blissful honey from your rivers of thrills which gives me fever in haste
Shocking seizures of rolling waves until we reach the shore of fulfillment
Understanding the oil of sweetness you bring that fills me with contentment

I'm beseeching all the elements of this hurricane of divine love
Winds, floods, thunder, lightning and rain hover around like a dove
Come with electrifying sequences of bestowing kisses on my lips
Bring me to the place of utter submission of powerful love which rips
Let me become lost in your bountiful and majestic gifts of elevation
Oh, hurricane of love, hold me in your arms in an unspeakable fashion.

A place where we endeavour to keep until time will be something of the past
A beautiful union we must cherish as it seems to be here to last
So let's continue with our discovery of fervent arousal of undying love
Entwined in the circle of a magical halo coming from above
The rainbow arched in the heavens each colour representing adoration
Limitless sunsets enveloping the hurricane halted with captivation.

Sonia Lahrar

THE ENGLISH CIVIL WAR, NORTHAMPTONSHIRE AND LEICESTERSHIRE

My name is John Middleton, born in Lutterworth,
A cavalry officer, underneath the
Leadership and flag of Prince Rupert,
A staunch royal supporter of
King Charles I.
The civil war had become contagious since
It began in 1642, with families battling each other,
With death and destruction on the battlefield,
With army life a constant struggle for survival.
It was now June 1645 where both armies stood,
Facing each other on the field at Naseby.
Fear crept through the ranks on both sides,
As soldiers, pike men and cavalry assembled themselves,
Where royalists cheered for the glory of the King,
One could see the glint of sun, reflected off the breast plate armour
Of the roundheads in the far distance.
On this memorable fateful day.
While Cromwell could be seen, rallying his men, upon
His white charger, a dashing figure, who now
Had order amongst his New Model Army troops.
The day progressed with much carnage and bloodshed,
But all was in vain as the King was ushered off
The battlefield as his loyal troops were routed,
Where now it was every man for himself,
As survivors fled and escaped in all directions.
I fled the aftermath of the battlefield, when all was lost,
And picked up a terrified women, from the baggage train,
And rode fast to the hamlet of South Kilworth,
Walcote and on to Misterton Hall, for I knew
Within my heart that there would be, reprisals.
I sweated profusely, where defeat had become
Unbearable to say the least, our cause was finished.
We arrived safely at Lord Peppington's imposing hall,
An important friend and ally to the King,
Where the saddle was removed, and my faithful horse
Was put into pastures around the estate.
The young woman that I had valiantly rescued,
Was named Lydia Thomas Grove, who was soon
Put to work as a maid in the kitchens, and was
Told to keep her mouth shut.
Where I was placed inside a priest hole, a secret hideaway,
Behind wooden panels in the library,

Two hours had elapsed when roundhead soldiers
Were heard and seen entering the estate of Misterton
Their horses panting wildly for breath,
A thorough search was made as cold sweat trickled down
My brow, I could hear the soldiers tapping on the walls
And shouting abuse at Lord Peppington and his loyal staff,
With the sound of musket shot being fired, which seemed
Like an eternity. Four hours I remained quietly entombed,
Hoping I would not be discovered.

A Civil War Poem
The Lost Battle Of Naseby

To his peoples of England,
The king accused of treason,
Where the death warrant was read,
The King who would lose his head,
As his cavalier army fled,
Where England bled
On the battlefield of red,
Over a thousand men are dead,
O cruel defeat, o defeat,
Upon his majestic royal seat,
No longer to reign,
As the divine right of kings,
Upon the Whitehall Palace scaffold,
The banqueting hall, the axe did fall,
Chopped off, a royal head so bold,
Where his supporters fired a leaded ball,
A martyr to the English crown
The King did weep of all his keep
In memory of an Oxford town,
The defeated King who had sympathies
To the Catholic cause
Did frown at his demise,
As Lord Oliver Cromwell arose,
Like a fury in the skies,
As Prince Rupert fought on gallantly,
The lost battle of Naseby.

I vehemently hated the roundheads,
For they had slain my only brother, by hanging him
On false pretences, this the horrors of war.
To my surprise I was eventually released from my
Cold stone prison, relieved that I had outwitted
Cromwell's troops. Lord Peppington soon brought me a
Glass of fine French wine, as we all toasted our freedom. I asked of
Lydia, and she was brought to me, with tears of happiness, where

We both hugged each other for a while.
She told me she was from the village of Cotesbach, not far from
The Watlin Street, where the wooden gibbet stood.
And she had been employed, orphaned out as a fish girl,
Who would catch trout, pike and carp from the local streams,
To feed the armies of the royalists.
Later we heard stories of Lutterworth being searched,
High and low by Cromwell's men, with strict orders to
Shoot, and hang all deserters, sympathisers and royalists,
Who may be apprehended therein, with puritan proclamations
And pamphlets given out to the citizens, by order of
The English Parliament of the grave consequences of
Continued support for the royal Monarch,
It was a known fact that three fellow officers
Who served under King Charles I,
Were cleverly hidden inside the Cavalier Tudor Inn,
Where after they made their good escape.

I had been so preoccupied within the Cavalry, that
I had not noticed this remarkable young girl before,
In my own baggage train and she swore that
She had virtually been kidnapped by the royalist army.
I gazed at Lydia for some considerable time,
She was sweetly compelling to the eyes,
The symmetry of her face and body,
Dark like ebony, a beautiful woman of the stars themselves,
Like angels, on Beauty's wings,
Upon cloudless skies.
The church bells rang out across Leicestershire
Of Cromwell's departure, who now had
The city of Oxford in his sight, and other royalist strongholds,

Four years elapsed, when news filtered through that our beloved
Monarch had been executed by Oliver Cromwell's
Parliament, a sad day for England, where we said prayers
Inside the chapel at Misterton Hall.
His beheading caused great concern amongst royal supporters,
Who cursed Cromwell's meddlesome nature into State affairs.

The civil war had spoilt King Charles I reputation,
Where Parliament blamed him personally for every
Cruel and murderous effect, on and off the battlefield.
Madame Lydia had now blossomed into womanhood,
Mature and innocent, a child of the universe,
Who one day would become a gentle woman of the crown,
With the eventual restoration of King Charles II.
We were both extremely happy and we had fallen in love,

Where we shopped in Lutterworth high street,
Where Madame purchased, velvet slippers, underskirts,
Fans, silk neck scarves etc, and I surprised Madame
With an engagement ring of our fourth coming marriage.
Later we picnicked, in a secret location on the estate
At Misterton Hall. With a backdrop of trees,
Cedar, oak and weeping willows,
Across the manicured lawns, with pink and white blossoms,
Their beautiful petals scattered as far as the eye could see.
Where we left our thoroughbred horses tethered to the iron railings,
As I prepared the picnic hamper, with wine and blanket,
The great imposing house stood in the far distance,
Idyllic, a vista of paradise, while enjoying each other's company.
Madame, was lovelier then ever upon this hot July day,
As I spied her natural beauty, methinks Lydia is greatest
When loved, thy lady of muse, I whispered her ear,
With love poetry, as Madame penned her day diary,
As birds flew and sang across the English landscape.
We both kissed underneath Heaven's glorious canopy and skies.

Cromwell died, a puritan soldier,
Believing in God and country, that the war of attrition,
Was perpetrated by King Charles I,
Where he had sold his soul to foreign powers.

The church bells rang out across fair bright England,
An end to Cromwell's reign,
With the restoration of King Charles II,
Our glorious reigning monarch,
A demonstration of liberty and unity.
Who wears the Crown Jewels.

Eventually we were united,
As Madame Lydia stepped forward,
Dressed in satin, sequins and pearls,
Befitting an aristocratic marriage
At St Mary's Church, Lutterworth,
I a seasoned soldier of war.

James Stephen Cameron

TOUGH LOVE

The world revolves and duly changes
Time moves on and rearranges.
Love leaves our souls bereaved and blind,
Impressing patterns in our minds.
Wise men offer wise, old words.
Fools sing songs we've never heard,
Little folk deliver hope.
And some see life as one big joke.
All are special, each are rare,
Measured by the folk who care.
Judges judge and mothers worry,
Fathers father – 'Hurry, hurry!'
Teachers teach what they are told,
Youth lives and loves and leaves the fold,
And what to be as they grow old?
Stormy weather leaves us scared,
Yet sheltered by the ones who've cared.

I love as I have loved before,
And now I open wide the door.
But it is fair to put aside
The love inside and walk outside
As no one touches me as you that came before.
The pain has eased. The scar it never goes away.
With words they tell me it is yet another day.
But who are they, those voices making words?
Their words don't heal the wounds
Or fill the lonely times. Love is all that can
So forward now I go to meet the world outside
And pride says, 'Yes I can!' I can live,
I can love, I can care! I'm proud and strong
So I go on. But still there's no one there.
The hope is now that those who've cared
Before are there to love and care once more.

Joan Elizabeth Blissett

WHITTINGTON

Turn again, you thief of night
You prowler, howler, footpad
As light as air, without a care
Turn again, as you reach your prize

You cut-throat beast with sharpened claws
Your cunning mind. Your larder full.
You stalk the shadows with bright eyes
You watch your mark and then you pounce.

Turn again, you reprobate, uncaring
You stalker, hawker, thuggie.
Slitted eyes, stiletto knives.
Turn many times before you kill.

You are just as inclined to walk away
With tail in air insouciantly
Leaving destruction in your wake
To lie in sun and wash your face.

Sue Daubeny

CAGED!

Locked up like an animal, no one to help
Alone in despair, great sadness felt
Dignity gone, evil took it away
Surreal situation, is it a play?
Anxiety, lurking, slowly suffocating me
No one to help break me free
Free from the shackles draining all that's sane
Crushing pride, long-lasting pain
Summon inner-strength to overcome my fear
Break free of the evil as darkness draws near
I spot my chance to run from Hell
Crisp, cold night full of deathly smells
Body's riddled with terror, adrenaline's rising high
Run as fast as I can, I at least need to try
Breathing's getting heavy, legs tiring fast
Heart pumping out my chest I feel I'll never last
Not far to go I can't bear to look back
One last desperate push, keep myself on track
Evil's closing in, but you're not getting me
Karma will get you in the end, just you wait and see.

Michelle Hardie

2012

The government advisor smiles
A satisfied smirk
As we think to ourselves
What a burke!
The policies wash over us
Each one designed to be
Another hurried development
Which awaits a tragedy.
Targets come thick and fast
Nail your colours to the mast,
The economic ship starts to sink.
As the whirlpool sucks us in
We fight and gasp for air
A drowning pair,
Spewed out the other side
It's not an easy ride.
But we have tested ourselves before,
As the light beckons us to the shore,
It's the beginning of a new day
Welcome to the blue ray.

Janet Rocher

THE CAT'S WHISKERS

On a bright and beautiful moonlight night
Two she-cats were scrapping on a garden wall.
Who is going to win? Who is going to fall?

They are fighting over Jim the ginger Tom.
Such a handsome cat, virile and strong.
They are not the only ones to fall for his charms.
The one way to get his attention is to stay aloof, serene and calm.

He is a cool cat, thinks ahead
Lives in the fast lane, puts others to shame.
He is crafty and clever and endeavours to make life easy for himself.
Has no intention of staying in the background, alone and on the shelf.

He will choose you, not the other way around.
His paws are firmly ensconced on the ground.
And so watch your step girls when dealing with Jim.
There is only one winner here and it's him.

Sylvia Papier

132

THE TIME

There's a time to look up,
And let go of your fears.
There's a time to rejoice,
Amidst all your tears.
The way may seem uncertain,
And the path hard to take,
But lean on His hand,
He makes no mistake.
He will lead you and guide you,
Each step you can follow,
But wherever you go,
Do not leave till tomorrow.
We all have our problems,
The way not seem clear,
But open your heart,
And He will draw near.
Lay at His feet,
Give your troubles to Him.
Bring Jesus into your life,
And let rejoicing begin.

Jackie Allingham

NON JE REGGRIET RIEN (NO REGRETS)

In the darkest
Still and image
Observed with emotion
I reflect
On a time of love and lesson
That brings new softness
Deep respect – for experience –
Oft the teacher
To have happen or befall
With dynamic due attention
I gave my best –
I pledged my all
The wheel rotates in balance
A sensitive rhythm –
Shifts and slows
Confides me to transition
As with a retiring tide I flow.

Irene Gunnion

902 DAYS

On the 1st day, he arrived
In a place so far from home.
He unpacked his things
And spent his first sleepless night

For tomorrow would bring him
A new beginning, a new life
He would teach at the university,
Passing his knowledge on to the young.

The 2nd day brought him
A new start, fresh potential.
He made his way to the campus
Where unknown wonders awaited him.

The 10th day presented insecurity.
Around him his colleagues and students
Seemed more settled and content
Than he did in a moment.

On the 56th day he met Julia
He finally felt something about this place.
He'd never felt that way,
Never for someone in his life.

Over the next few days
He summoned up the courage
To ask if she wanted to meet up.
Time stood still for him when she said yes.

The 78th day came bright and calm.
At lunch he met Julia in the park.
They talked and ate amongst the scenery.
Everything was perfect, still and quiet.

It was only a matter of time
Before they became a couple.
The university was a haven for affection.
Days passed like threads on a breeze.

On the 100th day, he realised
That he was deeply in love.
Nothing else mattered.
He cared not for family or friends.

It was quite unsurprising
That when she left him,
He was distraught and angry.
A great chasm opened in his heart.

The days before him seemed dark.
They were long, strenuous and cold.
He felt himself disappearing
Into a world of darkness and insanity.

On the 902nd day
He left for a new job.
Heartbroken, he looked back.
On the days that stretched.

Things had changed a lot.
Since the 1st day so long ago.
How everything then was strange and new.
Now his world was so much different.

Harrison Hickman

THE FURY

When the words are violent
When the future's bleak
When the vision's blinded
It's then the right shall speak.
My voice is often loudest
And my feeling clear to all
I can hold back my fury no longer
At the sights which do appall.
My clenched fist holds tightly
As my pen scratches the page
To unleash this burning anger
Is to fill the void with rage
How fierce my eyes are burning
How hard my heart does beat
To berate this aching frustration
Smashing subtle and discrete.
I can hear the storm is coming
And the war is approaching soon
Prepare the road for winter
And meet the blood-red moon.

Cassandra Dalton

BURNING QUESTIONS

'Did you love me on the night you proposed?
Did you really love me?'
'I loved you.'

'Did you love me on our wedding day?
Really love me?'
'I loved you.'

'Did you love me. You often said it over the years?
But, did you really love me?'
'I loved you.'

'Did you love me with soft spoken words when you were ill?
Did you truly love me?'
'I loved you.'

'Did you love me when in trouble and wanted sympathy?
So, did you really love me?'
'I loved you.'

'Did you love me when happy and contented?
Was your love true?'
'I loved you.'

'Did you love me as in your dying breath you whispered it?
But, did you really mean it?'
'I loved you.'

'Did you love me as I held your hand and watched you slip away?'
'Did you really love me?'
'I loved you.'

'Yes. I believe you did love me and in return I loved you.'
'Yes, I loved you.'

'Your love was deep, sure and understanding.
You really did love me.'
'And I loved you.'

Valerie Tedder

PHAELANOPSIS

Tall and slender
Purple splendour,
My spectacular orchid.
Fashioned like a pyralid.
Bowing in a gentle curve,
Graciously prepared to serve,
Should an insect choose to settle
On her veined and glowing petal,
With a golden draught of nectar.
Bidding him now to inspect her
Pollen-dusted golden centre,
Set out for an insect tempter.
For in paying court to her
He becomes her messenger.
Strange to consider all this beauty
Exists but for such mundane duty.
Each purple floral diadem,
Balanced upon its fragile stem,
Created so some insect pleases,
To help unwittingly the species,
Thus guaranteeing reproduction
By a process of seduction.
Tall and slender
Purple splendour,
My spectacular orchid.
What your subtle parent did
Brought you into glorious being.
The perfection that I'm seeing
Is to me aesthetic pleasure.
Such delight one cannot measure
Though your purpose may be dull,
Oh, but you are beautiful!

John Goodspeed

POETRY RIVALS 2012

Poetry rivals – an interesting idea
Or something that appeals to me
Everyone should try it
To see how good they could be
Rather than just sitting there
You just pick up a pen

Really set your mind to it
Imagine the words and then
Very soon you'll have a poem
As good as you've ever written
Like the one you're reading now
So then you'll have the bug – you're bitten

To me it came quite easily
Whilst wondering what to do
Every time I am sitting now
No matter what I do
Themes for poems just come to me
You really have no choice

Take a pen and write them down
Well let's give this poem a voice
Even something simple
Like a poem for a child
Very often turns into
Everything that's wild!

Michelle Agnes Broadbent

A BIRTHDAY PARTY

Think of the hours to prepare
For a birthday party,
The things to buy for the feast
The decorations to put up,
Something's missing for us.

Think of the ho-ha of it all
The tiredness and fatigue,
The hours of preparations must give
A fine turnout for all finally,
To be at this splendid affair.

So the Diamond Jubilee celebrations
60 years of being on the throne,
Must have surmounted to some
For this fine celebration,
60 years of the Queen's reign.

Trevor Poole

NOW WHERE SHALL I START

I am encouraged to be a scribe
Words will not enter my brain
Try as I might. I just don't get the vibes
Are my efforts all in vain?

Not much of a scholar I do profess
What can I pen that will be of interest?
Everyday life? Nature's beauty? Feelings of love?
I will need inspiration a bit of a shove.

Can I put into words what I'm trying to say?
How to capture beauty that I see each day
Will my words paint pictures of everyday life?
Can I show how love stabs through the heart like a knife?

There are many before me who have penned what they thought
So perhaps to try I ought
To paint a picture with words from the heart
Now, where shall I start?

Sandra Gorton

BRIEF ENCOUNTER

On a gantry in Belfast, the great ship takes form
In frozen waste, off Greenland's shore, the iceberg is born
Dazzling, pristine, multi-facets glistening
Aimless, mindless, diamond-hard, diamond-bright
Caught up in the current off the coast of Labrador
South, towards the grand banks, it journeys on.
Long, white furrow, the great ship's wake ploughs across the ocean
Elegant, is she, with gilt and filigree
Ice crystal droplets on ornate chandeliers
Sky ablaze with star-fire, cold and mirror-clear
The cosmos looks on as the fatal hour draws near.
A shape looms in the darkness; a frisson of dread
The lookout cries a warning – 'Iceberg! Right ahead!'
Stately, majestic, queen of the sea
A meeting of titans, the iceberg and she,
Steel meets ice, a glancing blow
An instant in eternity
The iceberg bears a scar of livid red.
The great ship is swallowed by the mighty deep
No more than a plaything for the ocean's whim
Broken, she lies in the graveyard of the sea.
Unheeding, unknowing, the iceberg drifts on
Dwindling, diminishing in the warm Gulf stream
Merging with the ocean, into oblivion.

Leyna Hunter

JANUARY

Looking down on the dim lit street
The emptiness and silence
Made my isolation complete,
Two cards from Christmas past
From usual greetings were missing.
Aunt Fanny departed peacefully
A smile upon her face.
Friend Chad in his prime
Crashed out in sorry state.
After a hearty breakfast
My spirits began to soar
As I contemplated my blessings
Instead of life no more.
I earn enough to pay my way
My needs are not excessive.
Envy is not in my mind
Or material goods to cherish.
Imagination fills the void
Of all that's gone before.
Poetry led it must be said
A new world to discover
In historical prints, children's books
Short stories and a novel.
Blessed am I with words to try
To justify my being.

Robert Fallon

CRICKET IN ENGLAND - AN ACROSTIC

C   oaches cannot make a batsman learn his art,
R   unning up and down cannot be learnt at home.
I   nnings need to last all day to build a score – no use being
C   aught or bowled or stumped too soon.
K   eepers need to learn to be alert to take a diving catch with
E   ase – and hold it in the gloves.
T   est matches ought to last the full duration – four or five long days.

I   ntrepidity and fortitude are what the captains need,
N   o use being all out by first day evening.

E   xcitement for the crowds is all important, and they
N   eed to feel involved in what is going on.
G   enerous applause may greet a hat-trick – but why do batsmen let it happen?
L   et laziness with practice be forgot –
A   fter all, carelessness in judgment just will not do.
N   o one wants a run out early in the day.
D   aring and adventure will be needed to keep the sunshine warm and fresh.

Gwilym Beechey

A BIRTHDAY FEAST OF FOUR DAYS!

It was her day!
It was her celebrations!
We were allowed to watch
and to take part by lining routes.

It was her 60th!
It was her Jubilee!
We were witnessing her reign
of all 60 years completed happily.

It was a weekend!
It was an era of history!
That we should celebrate the Queens'
Diamond Jubilee in such lavishness.

Pamela Poole

I'M NOT TOO OLD YET!

I've reached the September of my life
That is what I am led to believe
But they will have to think again
When they see what I have up my sleeve.

I flew to Las Vegas on my own
I didn't win a fortune it's true
But I did fly over the Grand Canyon
It's what us 'oldies' do.

Twice I went up in a hot air balloon
To celebrate my 75th birthday
Climbing in and out of the basket
Not elegantly, if I'm honest, I have to say.

I have written two books of poetry
With another book on the way
I confess I have trouble with my computer
But I will sort it out one day.

I'm off to Scotland later this year
With jeep safari thrown in
My eyesight isn't as good as it should be
But I'm sure I will see the deer and its kin.

I don't move around so quickly
As I used to do before
But there are still so many paths to walk
And many new places to explore.

Although I'm on the downward slope to 80
I still have much to say and do
I haven't reached my September yet
In fact, I feel as good as new.

Mary Millar

PUDDLES

The child sits in a puddle
Caused by her pain
And stares at the image
Reflected before her
Of a woman, in the rain.
She watched as it caressed
The tears as they fall
To join the puddles
In which she sits.

But no one is behind her
No one else at all.

The women stands in the rain
And it joins the tears,
As they fall,
And unite in the puddles at her feet.
Yet no one sees her endless fears,
Or the searing aches of emptiness
That these tears evoke
For she cannot yet see the child
Though, she feels her pain,

No one is below her
No one else at all.

Yet should their tear
Stop falling
Where then goes their innermost soul?
So cry on the child,
Weep on the woman,
Cry until all fears are stilled
And all pain cried out.
Then, only then, can they truly end,
And child and woman
United at last,
Cry peace, everlasting peace.

Elizabeth Saunders

PARADISE POETS

Paradise poets with love in their eyes
Dreamlands with sailboats and full of surprise
Candyfloss maidens with lacy blue gowns
A fool on a bicycle peddling to town

Sunbeams and sailboats sailing from shore
Windows that lookout on scenes love armour
Silly boys surfing on sands full of sprite
Dreamers and prophets with their thoughts full of grace
Kisses in love land where memories are made

Faraway places with strange sounding names
Children at play with happy free games
Sandcastle valleys with flags flying free
Shell bays and stud lands just by the sea

Hills that explore the beautiful scene
Lollipop dreamers with grace in-between
Forests and enchantments that send you to space
With a gift in your hand and a smile on your face

In a tumbledown shack in a glade by the sea
Where pastures are blessed, where rabbits run free
Where the sun shines there daily
And the moon scores at night, with stars to delight
What a heavenly sight

Simple life's flowing with happiness realms
Nursery rhymes alleys with tropical palms
Gypsies in vardos with chavvy's to spare
Beautiful maiden with long flowing hair

A tale of two cities to delight you each day
One love to last as you kneel down to pray
A forest of words that flow from the heart
With no wordily gossips to make you feel smart

A kiss in the moonlight with the stars twinkling free
A message from God written only for three
In paradise alley where wolves never tread
There's a candle to hold and light you to bed.

Raymond Wills

MI BRUVVER 'ATES ME

Mi bruvver really 'ates me
Cos of what I did
I got 'im in trouble
When I were just a kid
He left me outside a shop
He went in on 'is own
To get his self some pop
Said that I were getting none
Told me afore he went in
When he came out I 'ad gone
I weren't where I shudda bin
He wun't go 'ome to tell me mam
Lad next door 'ad to call
An' tell 'er that he'd lost me
An' daren't come 'ome at all
Int' old manor 'ouse at top at hill
He said that he were hid
He said that he were really scared
Becos o' what he did
They went up t' police station
Where there I sat ya see
Sitting ont police counter
Wi' a great big cup o' tea
He never 'as forgiven me
It's very hard to say
He were twelve an' I were two
The day I ran away.

Patricia Lee Sheen

LIFE

Life is just a moment in time
Never standing still
Like the countryside sublime
Viewed from a yonder hill

Restless as a running stream
That falls from mountain high
Endless like a dream
Like a cloud up in the sky

Life will go on
Never will it cease
Till time itself has gone
And we rest in eternal peace.

John Mangan

PAINTING PETER

An easel sprouted from his head
He was alive, he wasn't dead
And was sitting as still as he could be
For a portrait class, right in front of me.

I've drawn his fingers like a bunch
Of things you like to peel and munch,
His glasses are sliding down his nose
And if you're not careful your perspective goes.

Now it's time for coffee and a chat
And some funny stories about a cat
Who was buried alive while thought to be dead
And three days later with muddy tread
Appeared on the window sill waiting to be fed.

A simple person then enquired,
'How did he get out of his furry tomb?'
'How would I know,' I replied,
'I was watching my tele' in the front room!'

Rachel E Joyce

TALES OF DEBAUCHERY

I feel sleazy and dirty and reckless
My bottles and women are topless.
Red wine on white sheets.
My girlfriend is caring and loving.
My lover is everything else.
Cold and mysterious, and irresistible.
The best things are forbidden.

As we kissed for the first
On the edge of the course
We were judged by the trees:
They were threatening but
We nevertheless nestled near,
Teasing twins and thistles –
Luxurious wind swept our hair
In the wilderness –
And we became convinced they were disciples
Gathered to hear our instruction,
Direction and tales of debauchery.

This is the height of impiety,
And I was very nearly on my best behaviour.
As I watch you wrapped in your faux fur throw
There's a look in my eyes that would give me away.

From the poisonous roots our displays
Were glamorous in a scruffy, roguish way.
We merged just to fade in a cloud of our smoke,
To smother our troubles for one night at least.

The flesh of this city is out of our reach
As we pick at the bones arm in arm.
And at night we were ravenous,
Your energy left me determined
To scar you with grievous bodily harm mementos.
Despite our intentions we couldn't contain
All our rawest excitement
With thoughts for the rest of the week.

This is all very scandalous,
And passionately reckless,
We suffer from solitude and obsession –
Dark and deep themes indeed –
And intent on pursuing this fraternisation
We feed the fire to ensnare a few souls.

I knew I couldn't abstain from your lure

If even I tried to resist.
There is most clearly a part inside
That can't say no to you, and doesn't want to.
I'm eager for chances to have my way,
For us to be carried in fierce and drunken fallacy;
Charged, wayward and outlaw-ish.
Lustful and charming, painful and primal, and fiery.
Just what can you do to me?

We include ambiguity in our intentions all day.
Though I know we evoke passion,
Provoke inspiration in each other.
And we'll do whatever we want . . .
It's like being chased by police
When you know you've got a faster car:
You just have to keep it on the road –
Wherever it goes.

Still our exchanges are sexually torturous
And I'll do my best to match you through all of this.
By you I'm enthralled and will stay captivated . . .
So distant and intense and dramatic.
We fight in lust until I overpower
Or succumb to your vivacity and dominance –
Squirming with desire.
We scrap and scratch and bleed –
So punishing, the most beastly
Actions to practice unleashed
On your body, to take you in tangles of envy and need.
But that is my mood . . . deprived for so long,
Starvation fuels vigour and greed:
Elements of an entity left skulking desperately,
Aching to feast and indulge,
Save it all for me.

The agony is the wait, the thoughts,
Of teeth and skin and tearing and moaning,
Ensnared . . . slaves to the dominance.
And skin is so slight and the blood spills so freely.
I will rise for morning if only to prove a resilience and tenacity.
Test me as far as you think I can take it, then further.
Such ferocity, no sign of half-measures
Will satisfy everything, but fire fades –
I'll come back for more
To reproduce this iniquitous bond
In maddened blind want, as creatures unforgiving
To the point of one sharp, pouring frantic night.

Throughout I pounce and strike and cry,
You and I are bare and desperate.
There is nothing else. Just restlessness
And then ensuring satisfaction,
I can't feel where we begin or end.
But we are crazed in the moment and physical.
I don't have all the answers.
Help me fill in the gaps, my scratches sting,
My sheets are bloody, throat is wounded.
I'm scarred by you and you're all over me.
I don't want these scars to go away.
For blood there is a little, quite a pattern,
It clearly seeped from flesh instead of streamed.
On my side of the bed.
We could easily add some colour, rich and bright,
I want some of yours on my covers.
By the end we are truly alive.

In the aftermath of us
I have that pang of emptiness, of longing.
Walks on the edge of a golf course on mild February nights,
Deep kisses, stark silences, long conversations.
There is eagerness, stir of passion, air of vitality.
Some urges won't go away.
I've a generous smile but a ruthless soul . . . you tempt me.
We could be bare beneath wine-soaked sheets, essence of sex,
Exploring new places in darkness.

Be insatiable, be real, I feel I know far more about you
Then I have a right to, but you let me in, every time so far
And it would break me if you didn't.
Let our feelings overflow, I know
You're so much more than everybody else can see.
We're more than spark-and-fade,
We'll never be an insignificance, it wouldn't suit.
Don't smother what we could have been,
Don't tell me you're the sort to let this die.
But if you prefer to see what you want to
Then turn a blind eye . . . it won't make us go away.

We both share this secret:
You can't back out, I won't back down, you wanted this,
You knew the stakes and now you're in it for the long haul,
Honey, I stalk your favorite haunts now and then
Until the moment I see you again.

Philip Nind

CATS

They take over laps for their afternoon naps,
Or curl up in your favourite chair,
And show no remotest regard for your protest;
It's best to pretend you don't care.

Promiscuity-prone when they're out on their own
And consorting with Toms that don't tarry:
One is suddenly four, or perhaps even more –
Their bahaviour is not exemplary.

Potentially vicious, not really malicious;
Disdainful of boundary fences,
They do not hesitate when they must defecate
Which, for gardeners, has consequences.

Discerning, fastidious, selfish, perfidious,
Nonchalant, haughty – on their terms or none;
Mystic, inscrutable, self-willed, immutable,
One's only interest in all is for one!

This one's adorable *that* one, deplorable,
Acting in ways that nobody expects.
A touch supercilious; less than punctilious
In their respect for our treasured effects.

When they must: self-reliant; when it suits them, compliant.
Belonging is not something they comprehend.
Aloof, condescending, remote and unbending,
Dismissive, permissive; companions, not friends.

Ineffably lovable; 'Heaven's above!' – able;
Torment of gardeners; bane of the birds.
Wily and willful and stealthy and skilful –
Just some of what's meant when we utter the words:
'That's cats!'

Alan Bignell

IN COMMUNITY

Act not like ant or bee
By instinct ruled,
But live by rational thought.

In collective peace
Be of one accord,
Sharing in life's every boon.

Unite to spurn the evil.
Fight only for that right
Discerned by all.

Live for today
But plan with forethought
To ease the pain of the morrow.

Draw upon faith
To penetrate the gloom
Of each passing day's events.

Rise up in unison.
Grasp each opportunity
The future brings . . .

John Allen Watts

MAKE HAY WHILE THE SUN SHINES

Make hay while the sun shines
I have heard them say
But how can they when the people
Have lost their way

So don't get led astray
And learn to pray
Then hopefully you will be saved
Come the judgment day, OK?

Sally Fovarge

PUPPET ON A STRING

Like a puppeteer you control my string,
Bending me to your every whim.
I twist and turn, try to resist, but remain in control of your devious fist.
Watch me dance, how I aim to please!
Your grip so tight brings me to my knees.
I dream of the day you let me go, and tire of this ridiculous show.
Just cut my string and free my will,
I long for when your fingers still.
The time has come to end this game, let the curtains close,
You'll remain unchanged.
For when you leave I hope you know,
How I long for the day you become the show.
Have someone bend you to their taste,
And wipe that smile right from your face.
May the strings wrap tightly round your throat,
And strangle you 'til you start to choke.
Revenge is just, one day you'll see
And rue the day you tried to control me.

Wynona Lodge

BEACON

The Jubilee moon, the golden orb of June
Lit the clearing at the forest's edge.
Charcoal embers in the beacon glowed,
While strident voices of the crowd travelled on the breeze.
In deepening shadows by the wood
A silent, solitary figure stood – took no note of these.
Westward looked with steadfast gaze
Viewed the downs for the Whiteshil blaze!
Then, upon the dark horizon
A distant, glittering matchstick flame!
A new sparkling, crimson conflagration.
It gave him hope, brought inspiration,
This thought, *human you are not alone*,
Before the spark goes out, hasten to pass this message on –
A blazing chain of light
Conquers all the shades of night.

Wendy Capel

BY THE POPPIED BANKS OF THE SOMME

Army knife, jumbled medallions,
And flint-lock rifle, the soldier cleans,
They shine, like precious jewellery,
On the rough-ploughed, bare, earthly seams.

By the poppied banks of the Somme,
Searching for peace? Searching for dreams;
From muddy brook, the river meanders,
Just like a war-wound's bloodied streams.

The fleeting time vanished,
As Somme's flood-water teems,
Upon its flow, now running slow,
Skewed, sinking, obliquely,
Audacious, sun gleams.

For the life-humbled battalions,
Worn down by Death's cruel, unholier scenes,
The conflict's fierce and grueling,
Like none before, it surely seems.

Lines are copied, thanks to the tome,
War strategy, the general gleans,
The musty book, described past commanders,
A strand of raw, battle-scarred themes.

Near fainting and famished,
Much shed blood, slaughtered fiends;
Tired troops behold their cunning foe,
Shrewd-thinking, discreetly,
Voracious, Hun schemes.

Lost troop's wife grumbled, 'Rebellion's
Unacceptable in teams,'
The written edict's ruling,
A base deserter, the rule of law deems.

For the King and for the Kaiser,
There are, as yet, no clear sunbeams;
Bloodied rivals, troops surrounded,
The gunfire blasts, the soldier screams.

Like shining, well-burnished,
Hand-polished, wedding rings,
All the Great War's fallen heroes,
Their merit, time's hindsight,
Loquacious, esteems –

Many strife-tumbled rapscallions,
Amidst all of these grim scenes;
Are apprehended, dueling,
Over who lives out their fondest dreams.

For the Prince and for the pauper,
The war wounds fester, under creams;
Studied Bibles, they're well-grounded,
The Hebrew Prophets wrote down reams.

Glad tidings swell, furnished,
Fanned Gospel, angel's wings;
Christ is extolled among all those,
God's Spirit's sublime, light,
So gracious redeems.

Andrew Stephenson

MEMORIES

In my garden of roses
I sit and reminisce
Of the days of yore
When hand-in-hand we strolled
Along the far-distant shore
The magic of our first loving kiss
When you promised to be mine

In a little chapel on the hill
We were wed, your hand in mine
You dressed in bridal white
As shyly you whisper I do
So we became man and wife
Hand-in-hand we walked
The road of life together
Through laughter, joy, and tears
These were our best years

You now doth dwell in Heaven
I am all alone
Awaiting God's calling to his realms above
Where we shall meet again my love
And in hand-in-hand together
Will tread God's halls of glory
In his eternal love.

Daisy Carr

LOST ON EARTH, FOUND IN HEAVEN

Tonight my love the tears like rain are falling,
And rent the hearts and minds and souls apart,
Within that darkest void left with thy passing,
Upon God's ocean a new life I must chart.

And through the hell and anguish and the torment,
I'll damn them all, what more can I say?
For night is guaranteed to bring tomorrow,
Yet life seems ended here today.

And yet I know you're there beyond the mortal,
To walk with me where silent footsteps fall,
And shadows cast on pavements by the moonlight,
Awakes my soul to answer to thy call.

And memories shall help me face each morning,
Upon the wind I'll hear you call my name,
And bridges bridged by bridges they will take me,
And loose the shackles that mortal life does claim.

Yet boldly will I tread the paths I wander,
Guided by thy spirit on my way,
God must have wanted roses in his garden,
So many precious blooms he picked today . . .

Tread softly then, await my final calling,
And as for me I know life must go on,
So many stars tonight were born in Heaven,
We watch them shining brightly, each and every one.

Joseph Brohee

OF MERCIES BREATH

'Tis stench of man may first befall thee
For kindred all in mud found trench,
Ask pity not for none will find ye
But sewer rats, where is the sense?

Cruel bayonet point his neck defiling
Small trace of blood there flowed on rim,
One downward surge 'tis foe departing
Spoke sergeants words, 'tis ye or him.
Pale eyes shone mine in equal terror
Face mirrored mine for both were young,
Dispatch this foe lad make not error
No prisoners take, 'tis battle won.

Sweet flowed a voice in heat of battle
Brief quelled of screams, did silence guns
And 'twas a voice unlike no other
Seemed weaved of smoke as softly sung.
If he were ye and you were other
This mother's heart 'twould surely break,
Son use him well or grieves a mother
Grant mercies breath for pities sake.

As soon as there, 'twas soft in going
In languid field but flowed in dream,
Still bayonet held the while unknowing
As captured foe there smiled serene.
For this song my own sweet mothers
This mercies breath he too had breathed
If song were mine or sang of others
Her words of love there set him free.

One clench of hand mud boots at scurry
For soft of lilt we both had heard
To stench of trench though wore not worry
For sang in head my mother's words.
If he were ye and you were other
This mother's heart 'twould surely break,
Ye used him well now grieves no mother
For mercies breath and pities sake.

If mercies breath sad world 'twas flowing
No mother's heart 'twould surely break,
If he were ye and you were other
An end to war for pities sake.

John Cates

LONDON OLYMPICS - PAST, PRESENT AND FUTURE

Land that was once devastated by bombs of war
With many an acre once covered by industry is no more
The UK has welcomed many guests from afar
Once this unloved area doth now shine like a star.
This end of London now transformed into a venue to gladden the heart
It was a long wait for London's Olympics to start.
The ambling and now attractive River Lea
So pristine for all to see.
A river that once oozed with the detritus of industry
Now a pleasurable scene for all we shout with glee.
Filth and all miscellaneous chemicals were once afloat
We can now relax and watch with many a passing boat.
Look back with nostalgia to our last Olympics in the twentieth century
Now with the twenty-first we have made a distinguished entry.
Look at this transformation with natural pride and joy
So let's shout aloud and be proud and not be coy!
When all the fervour of the Games has subsided
Let us a nation be united and not divided.

Wes Thammer

STEELS

Mild steel, the common kind,
Tinned for your tin can
Stainless steel, the rustless kind,
For the bread knife in your hand
Carbon steel, the cutting kind
Hard and tempered sharp
Tensile steel the musical kind
Makes the strings upon a harp.
Armour plate steel, the resistant kind,
That saves the soldiers' lives
Tool steel, the working kind,
This makes the screws we drive.
The kings of metals in industry are
Steels, steels, steels.

Peter John Morey

FEELING MY AGE

I was at a poetry reading, a festival promotion,
When a featured poet came up with a very curious notion.
I had done my turn, had drunk a bit, was growing comatose
When I heard him say, 'I'm thinking of you all without your clothes.'

I had a sudden vision of the people round about,
Some young and slim, some middle-aged, and growing rather stout
No longing fighting cellulite, just flabby, adipose –
Imagine all that surplus flesh without disguise of clothes!

He was young and dark and vigorous, and his poetry involved
The problems people talk about, but very seldom solve,
So he championed youth and colour, in addition he proposed
To strip away the mask from truth, see life without its clothes.

I suppose he thought if sins were bared, we'd see them, and be shamed
And by this means society was bound to be reclaimed,
But think of sin like cellulite – unpleasant, pimpled, gross . . .
Are you sure you've got the stomach to see that without its clothes?

I quite see the necessity to look sin in the face,
To strip my soul, assess my crimes, and suffer my disgrace;
But do I want to see the sins that others would disclose? It doesn't seem respectable – so please,
put on your clothes.

And there's another angle to the image you display:
How difficult to face the truth when masks are stripped away,
Or to contemplate reality – I should do it, I suppose.
But I'm middle-aged and nervous, so please, put on your clothes.

I will sit here and be counted when you man the barricade,
I'm unlikely to come with you, because I'm too afraid:
I'll listen to your poems, and applaud them at the close,
But I'll huddle in my corner, and I won't take off my clothes!

Elizabeth Parish

DANCING WITH THE STARS

Last night I flew up to the moon
And danced among the stars
On Venus, the Veleta, a minuet on Mars
Gene Kelly, with umbrella, led me on a merry dance
He twirled me round Uranus
Then he left me, in a trance
I sashayed onto Saturn, ran rings around the samba
Then moseyed down to Mercury
Quick-silvered through the mambo
Nijinsky was on Neptune
Where we danced a fine duet
His entrechat, our pas-de-deux,
My perfect pirouette.
On Jupiter I jived with John,
From Grease, my what a boy.
Round Pluto did the polka
I have never know such joy.
But suddenly, a shooting star
Came tumbling round my head
It sent me spinning down to Earth
Then I woke up in my bed.

Doris Critchley

LOVE IN THE THIRD AGE

There was an urgency that drove your kiss –
Now just almost dutiful, a touch of lip on lip.
Once your impatient strength demanded
My surrender to the body's sweet convulsion,
Like spirits into hot oil flamed – Though
Loving still, your arms strain for their hold.
Where once you leaned for love, now you
Must lean for strength – I have become a lover
Of a different kind, attending, comforting,
Fetching, feeding, holding your need in mind.
You must move alone, in ways I cannot follow,
Which, for a time, will lessen your distress.
I mourn the skilled, the ardent one, and tend
Love's gentle ghost, that once was hot and strong.

May Worthington

160

A STORM

My senses tingle with anticipation as I
Watch the dark clouds gathering overhead.
It's not long before the heavy rain begins to fall.
My skin is covered with a glistening
Sheen and my hair hangs in a frenzy from my head.

The cold, driving rain is like needles falling
Onto my fingertips as I raise my palms to the sky,
Which bellows in time to the
Electric aurora of lightning.

My skin shivers and puckers with ecstasy
As my storm rages over me.
Each tendril of lightning sending chills of excitement
Dancing down my spine.
The wind caressing my wet skin,
Making each hair stand on end.

I lift up my face and close my eyes,
Feeling the power of the storm pulse through me with every breath.
Each raindrop kissing my cheeks and running into the bare ground at my feet.

It is so loud out here, with the angry thunder and teasing wind,
Yet there is silence in my head.
All the usual thoughts, worries, cares
Nagging at my brain are gone – replaced
With this peaceful exhilaration.

I'm sure if I stand out here long enough,
I will become part of the energy of the storm,
But for now I must return to humanity,
To monotony, to mortality, to life.

Kayleigh Vidler

OUR WEMBLEY HEROES

On March 27th year, '94
Our team once again entered folklore.
They set out for Wembley on a wing and a prayer,
The Champs there were waiting, our team didn't care.
In the 26th minute, quick as a dart,
Dalian struck like a knife in the heart.
The clock's ticking away, the Lions hold the line,
It's relief, it's the whistle, the ref's blown half-time.
Time to reflect and hear 'Stan Boardman' jokes,
Back out onto the pitch, there's more to come folks.
The Champs bombard 'Bozzie', the shots number seven,
Deano thwarts Sealey, our fans are in Heaven.
Heart-stopping moment, Man U's making news
They pull a goal back, scored by Mark Hughes.
Our heroes dig trenches and protrude a resolute jaw
The Champs show their metal, the fans know it's war.
Time ticking away, there's a foul in the box
Deano places the ball and pulls up his socks.
Then strides up and blasts the ball into the net
Yes! This is the day we will never forget.
The whistle is blown, the battle is over,
The fans, the players and Ron are in clover.
This verse is from memory, I can always look up,
The Villa, our heroes, have brought home the cup.
(Thanks for a great victory lads).

Charlie Hughes

I SPIDER . . .

Daddy had his long legs
Mummy spider had them too
They discovered a new web site
For the things that couples do
Soon came little long longs
And when productive time is run
Go in search of Miss Muffet
For lots and lots of scary fun.

Trevor Vincent

GREBE WHARF

Two godwits flutter vertically,
shrieking in a wind
that whistles through my shirt.
A sitting grebe grunts raucously,
resenting my proximity.

I am a bipedal mammal
emitting fearful pheromones:
an intrusive summer visitor.
This is not my habitat.

The harrier in the reed line
stoops to seize a hatchling while
a kestrel 'lights upon a post
to rip her prey to sinew.
I'm ambivalent, thrilled and appalled.
Violence stimulates me.

A ram mounts a ewe in the meadow.
She goes on grazing.
You wonder if she noticed!
I am diverted,
and deep within me, coyly aroused.
Classically English, I suppress it.

Bill plunged, arc winged, a cob repels his offspring.
The coots squabble incessantly,
while I waste my time in introspection!
Is nothing serene on this mere?

I KNOW . . . !
I am homo sapiens –
ambivalent, indulgent,
anthropomorphic, intrusive.
I am a sentient, multi-facetted,
violently destructive mammal!

SO?

John Burman

LONDON FIELDS

There are green parrots chattering high over London fields.
Dem bad boy crooks are being culled
havin' dare wings clipped or hangin' low.
Jude's corner, where Stuie laboured on the bench to enlighten the long past caring, clutching his
strong bow for annihilation
eerily quiet
opposite the Cat and Mutton
now masquerading as; us-e-lot avec spring lamb.
'Vote Labour today,'
comes the cry from the poster daubed mobile husting
hasting toward the junction with Middleton Road.
Where a Tony and Cherie once made babies.
'I did,'
I shout into the heavily polluted Broadway Market lunch menu air,
'for far too long.'
The Thane of Fife a pasty made, the man of constant values a self-styled ambassador for a
peace:
New Labour speak for; filling your boots from both sides,
accumulates wealth beyond her wildest dreams
and they play: 'Catch us if you can.'
On a journey between their ever increasing piles of armour plated rank hypocrisy.
Now those crocodile tears for such a little piece of Bristol's waterfront seem well shed.
You can take the girl out of Merseyside
but you'll need more than a contrite Liver to cleanse that much red.
Foul is foul, fair is air.
Toffees might soon be cowering under blue-blooded, four-poster, feather beds.
Macbeths will be kings
until the great burdened come to fight that being done in their name
and we stand like those ancient trees in that English city field
Our party and our nation to reclaim.
Try and rest easy Stuart, proud comrade, lion mettled friend.
A socialist and a fighter, until the very end.

Alan Harman

AN EXCITING TIME IN 2012

In summer 2012 the year is unusual,
For the Euro Football, Wimbledon Tennis, Olympics and Queen's Diamond Jubilee,
On all of us (nearly at one time,) fall.
Usually a beanfeast quite like this doesn't come,
So for the spectators is bliss
The participants and organisers have a hard time,
Working like Trojans
Enjoyably (we hope) too
To bring excellent entertainment to me and you.
Cheers to everyone, and Prince Philip is well,
Here's to 91
An enjoyable task,
And the royal family have done and won,
With the devotion, love and proficiency awarding to us,
Our Great Britain.
A better time than 2012 summer is impossible.
The likes of this one-off summer can't be re-seen,
Except as a legacy on television,
That will be everlasting for future generations,
It'll forever foot the bill.
Cheers to all the royals, athletes, administrators, organisers,
And now a 'fit as a fiddle'
91 year old Prince Philip – hip, hip hooray to all of whom I mention.
Their devotion and love to ours and their own countries is sure to merit everyone's attention.
Three cheers to the good times in 2012!

Jean Helen Davy

DREAMSCAPE

I was knocked out cold
By your startling beauty
By your overwhelming hold
That threatened to claim me
To break me and to maim me
To name me and to shame me
Oh, but you cannot possibly know
How good that feels to me

I saw you a-glow
In the faded twilight
You were naked and you were gold
You were such a holy sight
And I was humbled
I was humbled by what I saw
You entered me through my eyes
And you ignited my soul
I was so excited
I was out of control

I watched you unfold
Like a lily
Like a rose
I said, 'Whither thou goest
I shall surely follow'
I watched you shine with the stars
And burn with the sun
The night was ours
For to be made undone

God you were divine
I looked into your eyes
You looked into mine
And I just knew
That I wanted you
And I had nowhere to hide

I was as one defeated
I fell at your feet and
You just glowed
You glowed
You glowed so brave and so free
With a light so bright
And so heavenly

You were naked
In all the ways a human should be
Like Eve
I thought that you were made for me
I thought that I was fated for thee
And you glowed so brave and so unapologetically

You were my Venus
You were my God
You were my Jesus
You were my holy dove
I was for you
And for you alone
And I was, and I was
And I was, and I was
And I was reborn

I was knocked out cold
By your startling beauty
I was awed completely
I was well and truly floored
I tried to win you
But loneliness was my reward
I was knocked out cold
By your startling beauty

And you say that you are busy
You say that you don't care
You say that you will meet me
But I just have to know where
Or when
And you say that you love me
My art and my poetry
But I pray thee, say that you love me
Yeah, say that you love me
Say that you love me
Say that you love me and then
Say that you love me again

I was knocked out cold
By your startling beauty
I was alone, I was stone
You were pure as can be
I was so alone
Before you happened to me

I was left standing on the ledge
Of hope and desire
I was left stranded on the edge
Of this thin tightrope wire
You were my teacher, you were my friend
Now, I'd gladly walk through fire
Just to see you again

Your love is a love with no real name
But I know how you feel
'Cause I feel the same
You know who I am
And you know what I am thinking of
You're my inspiration
You're my holy dove

And I miss you forever
Now that you're gone
And I long for the days
When I was your student
And you were my only one
And I was, and I was
And I was, and I was
And I was reborn

Yes, I confess
That I did dream of you
Just the other night
You held me in your arms
You held me there so tight
And I swear I could not breathe
When I saw your inner light

And I'll climb the holy mountain
And ascend the eternal stair
I'll climb right the way to Heaven
That I might find you there
Looking so beautiful and kind
So rare and so fair
I'll permit you to float forever
Over the ephemera of my every prayer.

Timothy Rosen

WI BIRTHDAY PARTY

Mabel Collins was the one in charge, she is president this year
She wanted something different and that's just what she got I fear
It started off quite sedately, with an entry glass of wine
And if it wasn't for the fancy dress, things may have worked out fine
But Jean tripped over Mary's bustle, then carriered right into Mabel
Who was filling up the glasses and standing at the table
The glasses did the Highland fling, the bottles took a dive
The look Mabel gave to Mary could have skinned her alive
The wine was flowing freely, but alas upon the floor
When invited guest the vicar walked through the door
The look on all their faces was really quite a sight
I really thought the VCO was going to die of fright
Later when the mess was cleared we played a game or two
A few very old ones, but some of them were new
We played a game of hockey with tea towel and walking sticks
We laughed until our sides ached, as good as any flicks
Our team tried to get some goals, tried very hard to win
But the only thing that we achieved was breaking Peggy's shin
When the ambulance had taken Peg away
Games were the last thing we wanted to play
We sat around tables to sample all that food
But didn't say Grace, which was very rude
For the vicar had said she'd do it, but we all forgot
I think all the committee will probably get shot
The VCO in state of shock looked very agitated
I really think our WI will be excommunicated
Our president in her cat suit stood up to cut the cake
Her wine soaked tail behind her trailing soggy in her wake
The toast was made in water cost the wine was on the floor
An evening to be remembered for evermore
When all the guests had duly gone, we huddled in committee
Chewed the evening over, said it was a pity
The evening hadn't gone as planned, in fact got rather out of hand
The next time would be better, on that we all agreed
Then said goodnight to each and all, and toddled off at speed.

Dora Watkins

SOLILOQUY

I met my man at sweet 16 just as I finished school
I fell so hard my mother said
'Oh don't be such a fool. The word is full of men
And so just take a look around
Don't pick the first bad apple that has fallen to the ground.'

But
He loved me, and he was my world; her words I did not heed
(If I could turn the clock back – what a different life I'd lead . . .)
So – I 'did my thing' and married him. I did the best I could
I worked two jobs in early days in order that he could
Begin his life in business (which had always been his dream)
Then we'd have lots of money and enjoy life to extreme.

But things went wrong the first time – then the second – then the third
We lost our home and lived in rooms, and yet, it's quite absurd
That I never did stop loving – never doubted him, you see
And even with three children the rent was down to me.

But I never let him down – was always steadfast, true and loyal
And (apart from satisfaction), I got nothing for my toil.
I worked a job from eight till five although I had small twins
Cos I always sort of thought *if one keeps at it – then one wins!*
But after twenty-four long years I'd gone to work one day
And discovered to my horror that while I was out all day
My husband was adulterous – he'd found a divorcee
Who was living off her 'ex' – and had more time for *mine* than me!

My world just fell about me, and I wished I could have died . . .
To think he'd spent our money – and of all the times he'd lied!
I packed his case and bade him leave (the lesser of two ills)?
I said, 'I hope she'll do the same, and like me – pay your bills.'

I had no time for counselling – I had the rent to pay
I had no time – I had no time
And he just walked away.

Inevitably
The sun rose, and another day dawned
And all the pain of loneliness returned
And yet – I didn't know that this might be
The start of a whole brand-new philosophy . . .

Still –
No more dreaming dreams, or scheming schemes;
The 'normal life' had split right up the seams.
From hereonin I seemed destined just to be
A lone spectator on life as it ought to be.

Sometimes I thought I'd never laugh again
And sure as hell I didn't like the game . . .

Yet
Children huddle closer in a storm, so
In consequence I never felt forlorn.
We learned to value health and simple living;
The art of hope when there's just love for giving . . .
I helped them see wealth comes in many guises
Material wealth (perhaps) a lonesome heart disguises?
Contentment at what is – not at what might have been
And still – through my childrens' eyes – the strength to dream.

But since that nightmare, some of the best times that I'd had
With simple freedom, more happy times than sad –
Eventually – the chance for me to simply be a mum – and to
Care for my dear parents till their Maker they succumbed.
And I never had the worry of the rent to pay, you see
And life got slowly better and (though lonely) – good for me
For although I wasn't rich, I was a happy soul – and free!

But I feared about the future, and ambition stirred in me.
My daughter flapped her proud young wings and left our family . . .

For reasons quite unknown, my 'ex' rejected our small twins
(They were only four years old when this sad tale begins)
He was full of empty promises – never gave them any time
In consequence of which I gave them twenty years of mine!
(Which is 'what it's all about') – and there is nothing I regret
But there's a nagging deep inside about the future I will get
Because I haven't got a home and (well – not yet!) I have no man
So I thought I'd get a job and try to do the best I can

And then one day – if I worked real hard (before I was too old)
I'd get myself a mortgage, and not 'stay out in the cold'
(Because 'living on the state' you are a 'have not' and you see
I just got discontented with life's hard reality)

Still – there's a happy ending to this tale of misery
'Cause I still enjoy my freedom and I'm happy as can be
It gave me time to write this rhyme – some inbuilt therapy
Because it felt like someone else – just anyone but me . . .

(Alternative ending)
Cos when you've had – then lost – most everything
And you really don't know why
It isn't very difficult
To just lie down and die . . .

Edna Sparkes

171

JUST A SUIT

Just a suit, just a suit, just a suit, just a suit
You may think I'm just another suit on the train
But underneath this dull, grey clad exterior
I could be Superman
I could have hidden talents
I could be the next Prime Minister

I might be just another fish in the sea
But against that statistical improbability,
I could be your Mr Right
I could be your shiny armoured knight
We could be dynamite

You might be a figment of my imagination,
But beyond the hypothetical,
There is every possibility,
That you and I,
Exist.

Oliver Sayers

BY INSTRUMENT

As I glance at the bar, the key to my relationship with you stares me in the face.
Recognising your lyrical movements, and wistful air, I remember the last time my hand cradled your slender neck,
Though your sharp tone reproaches my troubled psyche,
Things take a natural progression, as I long to hold your rigid form against mine.
Consumed with an aching hunger for perfection, I listen, feel, then understand the voice that resonates deep within your hollow belly.
Whilst plucked from obscurity, I now comprehend your mood and purpose,
And taking a stand, I study the manuscript one more time,
To manipulate each string adeptly, and sympathetically,
Then drink of your soulful melody.

Junie-Marie Flynn

LIMBO

It is a strange place, this Limbo land
Neither in real life nor no-man's-land
Parleying with a god long since departed
In a place of corpses carried and carted.

Holding out for another day
Of fear, disgust, anger, bitter dismay
Holding out for another week
Though the past is haunting and the future bleak.

Following orders given by a fool
I'm just an imperial country's tool
That will one day be smashed on the quagmire of France
And never had a choice, will not stand a chance.

And yet I find courage for my comrades
From long ago memories when I was a lad
Before a demon in me told me, 'Go to war
Condemn yourself to Limbo in Satan's kingdom's care.'

For it's the Limbo that pains me, the waiting around
Watching friend after friend die, till my death-knoll sounds
Not knowing how long, but knowing it will come
Like the army's march, the law-abiding drums.

It is a strange place, this Limbo land
No longer truly living, not yet in no-man's-land
Pleading with a god who left me to my fate
In the hands of a devil who's attending to this state.

But when the day comes, I'll unflinching, leave Limbo
To a happier place beyond, where I still pray I'll go
I only hope there's a god in the life I left behind
And the whole world hasn't turned to a Limbo of this kind.

Olivia Feilden

I WISH

I wish
Oh! That I could have one wish
To take us back in time
To the days of peace and quiet
And not of all this crime

When children played their children's games
And did not mug old ladies
And children down as young as twelve
Did not produce more babies.

Creed was not the pattern
And old folk weren't in fear
Of being thumped by some young yobs
To fund their lust for beer.

Drugs were kept by doctors
To cure a nation's ills
They weren't dished out is discos
In the form of deathly pills.

People married, settled down
And lived a normal life
Boys played with their fathers
And girls clung to his wife.

When Grampy died or Nanny
It was taken then as red
No old folk home for the one that's left
They lived with their children instead.

The law was there for all to see
With the bobby on the street
He knew the name of all the folks
That lived along his beat.

Food was good and wholesome
No balti and the like
The only ones delivering
Brought the groceries on a bike.

We did not need to worry
About locking up the home
Burglars picked the posher ones
And left the poor alone.

Lots of men were unemployed
Times were hard and money tight
But it did not make those people
Go out and thieve at night.

The war changed lives forever
And men were trained to kill
'Twas greed that started the conflict
And that greed is with us still.

Us older ones have run our race
And we hope we've done our best
The future of society
The young ones will rest.

So let them work together
And remember what they're told
'Cause one thing that is certain
Is one day they'll be old.

The tale they will tell their children
Will be of computers and the net
Of Pokémon and Gameboys
And all they didn't get.

They'll tell them that they're lucky
They weren't born in Grampy day
When all the children had to do
Was to go outside and play.

The greatest gift that all can give
And it does not cost a penny
Is that of giving just yourself
Not to the one but to the many.

Wendy Lynne Bryan

EXCELSIOR! VIVAT REGINA

Aloft a 'treehouse' in a safari park in Kenya,
The poignant news of King George VI's demise ruffled the air:
Dispatch came to 25-year-old Princess Elizabeth,
Who flew back home, re-born a queen, as grief encompasseth.
Verily, you may call it fate or chance or destiny,
But it's God who ordained Elizabeth to be Queen suddenly:
Uncle Edward's abdication after six months' sovereignty,
Made Prince Albert, her father, King George VI, lineally,
And her ascension a 'fairytale' of the TV age!
Wherein she pledged lifelong, her father's work to emulate.
Her Coronation was the first global TV event,
Heralding a very modern-style Monarchy's advent:
Queen Elizabeth II is 'Constitutional Monarch'
Officially, the Head of State, but run by government hierarch:
As a perk of royalty in the United Kingdom,
She's Head of State of multinational Commonwealth Kingdom
Carrying out political duties as Head of State,
Ceremonial responsibilities as the Sovereign Head,
Annual programme of visits in the United Kingdom,
As well as innumerable foreign tours in addition:
Now the longest reigning monarch since Queen Victoria,
And twelve prime ministers having come and gone during this era:
For sixty years, the most iconic person in the planet:
A constant Monarch for our lifetimes in every respect.
Starting the autumn years of her reign – the Diamond Jubilee Year
She delivered this deeply heartfelt pledge, very sincere,
'I dedicate myself anew to your service' – verbatim,
Echoing the vow she made clearly on her ascension.
Congratulations! Valiant Monarch – Sail on, oh Ship of State
Sail on for Great Britain and the Commonwealth, strong and great
Join we in celebrating your Diamond Jubilee with euphoria
Excelsior! Vivat Elizabeth II Regina; hurrah!

Welch Jeyaraj Balasingam

REGRETS UNANSWERED

I saw a silver cloud across the darkening sky
And wondered, was it you and did you ride
Over my life, an angel in disguise
Waiting for me to join you by your side?
For once you spoke of never leaving me
Comparison of moon with tide and ever-rolling sea
Now I, of no significance am lost
And left with life and all the guilty cost
To carry on alone with no one left to share
The gift that wasn't seen by us to value what was there
Now do you watch as from your new-found height
While I, a lonely mortal, wait now for the night
When I, in silence, can weep and try to find
The answers in the secret corners of my saddened mind.

Too late to question how, and what went wrong
Where we were going to or even coming from
Could things with thought, possibly have been better
Instead of living by the rules of every written letter?
Once dead the questions can't be asked,
Life's 'ifs' and 'buts' remain, but only in the past.
The evidence is faded, lost, forgotten, out of reach
As pebble roll and dash upon the waiting beach
Return, reviewed, rejected, out of mind
And so the answers that we want we will not find
So, I will dry my eyes, no longer reminisce
For that we never had we will not miss.
While you glide on, avoid the thunderous might
Gone, but not forgotten, into the waiting night.

Vanda Gilbert

NICE AIRPORT LOO

What a calamity
What a to-do
When I got locked in the
Nice airport loo.

We sat waiting patiently
To find out our gate
Hoping our plane was not
Running late.

I said to my grandson
Wait for me on this bench,
A bright little lad
But can't speak much French.

I went to the ladies
But oh deary me
That's when I got stuck
In the WC.

I knocked and I shouted,
'Aidez-moi, please,' I cried
A French lady promised
To find help outside.

A message came over
Said Gran was OK
But sadly for Zack
It was all in 'Francais'.

A security man came
And fiddled and twisted
But the lock stood firm
And completely resisted.

Terminal two is
So chic and classy
But it doesn't seem so
In the Nice airport karsi.

They took off the door
And set me free,
What a palaver
Just for a wee.

Zack greeted me
With a disdainful look
'I wasn't worried
I just read my book.

I've had a good holiday,
Nothing could spoil it
Even if Gran got
Stuck in the toilet.'

We hurried onwards
To our gate
Cos Easyjet
Will never wait.

Gate 26 is
A bit of a slog
When you've spent some time
In Nice airport bog.

Oh! What an experience
For a person to have
Incarcerated in
Nice airport lav.

Jacqueline Longley

THE JIGSAW OF LIFE

It's all about shade and light
Moods, places, time
This story of mine,
A fleeting glance between
A young man and a woman,
Drawn to spend time together,
Then a life as husband and wife.
The joys of watching our children grow,
And to know precious grandchildren.
Take them by the hand
And try to understand
The despair when more than one of them
Remained sleeping forever.
A kaleidoscope of colours, shapes,
Feelings of ultimate joy and sorrow.
A story for today and tomorrow.

Patricia Corry

MOONSHADOWS

Clouds across the moon's face racing
Throw strange shadows on the ground,
Why should these instinctive fear raise,
Flickering without a sound;
At one time, or in some places,
Yes . . . dangers might well abound,
But, apart from other people,
Real threats are now rarely found.

Ah! . . . but still, somewhere within us,
Lurk fears which our forebears bound,
With dimmed light dark superstition
Stalks us still – a spectral hound;
'Modern', 'educated' people
In dread wraiths of night-time wound,
Find that all their skill and knowledge
By deep terrors soon are drowned.

Me? . . . I feel the ancient stirrings,
Dread of unknown things surround,
But I also love night's hours,
Which with timelessness abound;
All Creation's vibrant rhythms
Still within *our* souls resound,
Fear not – just dance *with* moonshadows,
By the stars find yourself crowned.

David J C Wheeler

THE JUBILEE

This year is the Queen's jubilee
I was born in the same year as she
I too have a prince and a princess
My son-in-law and daughter
Who help me all they can
They do my garden
It's like a park
With lovely flowers and many a tree
No place for Adam and Eve to be
Because there is no apple tree.

Eileen Hannah

MY WORST NIGHTMARE

As I woke up one morning,
With blue skies all around,
I thought of the happy hours,
I will spend in the sun.

Before I could do anything,
I first had to do my chores,
But no matter how much I hurried,
It took longer than I thought!

Thank goodness, at last I had finished,
But I ached from head to toe!
So, it was time, for a hot cuppa,
And perhaps a shut-eye as well!

Alas, my nap took longer than expected
By which time, the sky had turned grey,
My mood was even darker,
At this change, within one day!

So, folks if the sun is shining,
And you want to relax in the sun,
Leave all your chores for the morrow,
For tomorrow never comes.

Maude Kiddle

COUNTRY

The countryside is special
Seeing people walking in the country.
Seeing ducks swimming in the water
And seeing the birds resting in the tree singing merrily
It is so restful walking hand in hand
Seeing different things you may have not noticed
Let us respect our country
Because it's a special place.

D Hallford

MY LIFE

A lot of anger inside of me
Like a volcano yet to erupt
I can't hear my screams
Got lost because of trust

I can't see but not blind
Even myself I can't find
Give me back my years I've left behind

The anger turns into a deep sorrow
No more care about tomorrow
You think I'm your own toy
Do whatever brings you joy

The little girl is growing up
Got her own way to go
Now you can't make me stop
While watching me leaving you.

Menna El-Baz

THE KING OF WESSEX

Who was it who came
To Salisbury Plain
In eight-seven-eight?
Why, Alfred the Great.

There are remains
Where he fought the Danes
And conquered them
With his well-trained men.

Through long grass and gorse
He rode his white horse,
Till a very steep drop
Made them all stop.

The Danes gave in
To the Wessex King
Where, instead of mayhem
He converted them.

Kathleen White

TEN MINUTES FROM TEARS

Tinny taste on my tangled tongue
It starts, dormant symptoms have begun
Restless sleep, I toss and turn, morning comes too early
Exhausted by noon
Thoughts, word patterns are obscure,
Riddles and random ideas pop into my mind
My chaotic ideas and daylight dreams corralled deep inside.
Outside, a faceless world of secret streets, and national normality
Far removed from tapping the window of insider insanity
Book a four minute consultation with fresh-faced locum GP
Frosty receptionist, horned Grim Reaper, is no help to me
Time maker, note taker, never a rule breaker this 'surgery gatekeeper'
My Maudling mood dragged down ever darker, ever deeper.
Ten minutes from tears all the time, dry tickly throat, responds well to lager and lime,
Swallow hard, involuntary blink, blink,
Barmaid's painted full moist lips, I order another drink
Strong cider, red or white wine, vodka shot
'Keep the change love,' cheers, as I finish the lot
Drinking buddies disappear, I'm left boozed up, doss down
Sleep late, miss another doctor's appointment
Dried up, tinny taste returns, sadness, disappointment,
Today I carry with me my irrational fears
Here I live, here I belong, ten minutes from tears.

Amelia Michael

HIS PRIZE

Wrapped in the dark enduring earth, my son
Lies sleeping forever.
We stand before the mound and bow to
Gods and bugle call. The young girl weeping,
Feeling the loneliness of a winter's bed,
Her covering strength lost in a
Dog-rose summer.
Such awful grief to patch with honeyed words
The wound-striped mind.

Winds mourn the feet below, whose shape
My heart has known and in the cellared gloom,
Comforting the rounded cheek, a small green tag
Rests like a pharaoh's jewel.
His prize, they said, is the day beyond tomorrow,
Your purse, the emptiness of noon.

Cynthia Lingfield

A MILLION DIAMONDS

A million diamonds danced upon the sea
The sky was inky black, the moon was high
Shedding its silver light upon the waves –
We stood entranced and marvelled, you and I.

A ribbon of jewels twinkled on the coast
Adorning hamlets nestling in the bays
The night birds wheeled and dived on silent wings
Reminding me of treasured happy days.

And so I reminisced beside the shore –
That diamond ring I purchased, all in vain
The evening sparked so many memories –
What would I give to see your face again?

But I still see you with my inward eye
For life was briefly kind to you and me
I won't forget the magic when, that night,
A million diamonds danced upon the sea.

Jonathan Bryant

184

'SUMMERLY' VIEWS TO AUTUMN

The sky from my window, is blue
Midsummer, drawing near too.
I'm not far off the sea, calling me.
To paddle my feet, in the sea, cooling off, you see.
The sand is warm, beneath my feet,
Sun been around early, what a treat.
Would liked to have stayed a bit longer
In this warm clime, am just running out of time.
No doubt holiday makers will be around
Enjoying the scene, I'll be bound.
This part of the coast, has a way of being, wet or fine
Windy or sea mist, clammy, cold or benign,
Weather men cannot always predict correctly, all the time,
Cannot bear to be away from land and sea too long.
Ancestors before me, brown and strong
Fishing or on land, were what they knew,
Me, being drawn between the two.
Managed to get out, seeing what's new.
Like fields of barley and wheat crops coming anew,
Saw them, with harvest approaching, and adieu.
Cattle on marshes, sheep and pigs around too,
Seasons change quickly,
Harvest over, fruit aplenty
Fishing season for herring? Not much now as
At beginning of century would be, harvest of the sea.
On land, factory open for sugar beet, called The Campaign.
Root crops, chaff for animals, and all the land's gain.
Hard to think about in summer weather
Please don't let it rain.

Mabel Deb Moore

CALM OF NATURE

With my last breath
Every soul to bless
I leave folk poetry
Enlightening them to reality
Gracious words with meaning
May folk find inspiring
Such be their future
By the calm of nature

If thou seek and believe
Troubled minds be relieved
There be a secret way in life
When found releases strife
A pleasant world discovered
In wonderment achieved
Thy every day be blessed
Every step thou descend

By the calm of nature
Thy heart feels pure
Heaven feels very near
Uplifting thee from fear
The sun shines brighter
Thy heart beats lighter
Every day begins with determination
Greeting everyone with affection

Offering friendship with a laugh
Every day thou master
Those days thou feel stress
Just take a rest
Close thine eyes
With feelings divine
All thy aches and pain
Discard from brain

Many joys come thy way
Keeping thee in array
When looking around
As the sun goes down
Glorious sunsets doth thrill
Before vanishing over the hill
There be silence thou endure
By the calm of nature.

Josephine Foreman

FOOTBALL WIDOW

Football! Football! Football!
Forgive me if I moan
But I'm a football widow
And I know I'm not alone.
'It's only ninety minutes,'
They say with a look sincere,
But don't you venture to believe them,
Watch them pour their second beer!
You know that ninety minutes
Is much longer than they say,
The match itself may be that length
But the extras will take all day;
With expert analysis, critique and comment
They take the game apart,
They pontificate, hold forth and posture
With the knowledge they burn to impart.

Still, really, it's not long to go now,
The whole lot will soon disappear
And TV will get back to normal
And leave the way open and clear
For soaps, documentaries, dramas
All the programmes to give me good cheer.
But – on no – what a fool! I'd forgotten,
How could I have been so remiss
What's that looming on the horizon?
Three weeks of Olympics . . . Oh bliss!

Ann Dodson

THE GREAT BRITISH WEATHER

We hang our washing out to dry
Underneath a clear blue sky
But moments later we start to frown
As clouds appear and rain comes down

The Great British weather –
It keeps us on our toes
So what's it got in store today –
For certain, no one knows!

The rain is playing its usual pranks
Rivers all over are bursting their banks
No cause for concern as sandbags are free
But we're already flooded, so they're no use to me!

Now we have a strong northerly breeze
And the temperature plummets by 15 degrees
We're told it's the jet stream that's mainly to blame
And that's why two days are never the same

Global warming makes headline news
Scientists tell us their gloomy views
Ice caps are melting and deserts are growing
Yet here in 'Old Blighty' it carries on snowing!

On those rare occasions when it turns hot
We run short of water – believe it or not
Dried up streams feed empty dams
Moorland fires and hosepipe bans

Ice cream sells out and railway lines buckle
It's hotter than Egypt – it makes us all chuckle
We raise our hats to the people of Spain –
Who manage so well with so little rain

As winter arrives we face a big freeze
It's colder than Russia – we all cough and sneeze
After one day of snow – everything stops
Road salt runs out, as does food in the shops

Trains become stranded and planes can't be landed
Disgruntled commuters become most off handed
A state of emergency, what a kafuffle
Wrong kind of snow, so we'd best find a shovel!

Above us now lies – a thick foggy shroud
The Met Office tell us it's fair weather cloud
They say they are sorry – they're doing their best
Then a force ten gale rattles in from the west

In the far distance we hear claps of thunder
It is coming our way – we do start to wonder
Lightning starts flashing and hailstones come crashing
Bank Holiday again – now isn't that smashing!

It's what we'd expect of our unique weather
Just as unstable and fickle as ever
We're not downhearted – in fact we're quiet jolly
Cos when we go out, we just put up our brollies!

It occurs to us then, whilst dodging the puddles
That all British seasons seem to be muddled
But it's been the same since records began
So make most of the sunshine whenever you can!

We close with our washing – it's still on the line
If it doesn't dry soon we shall run out of time
It's taken much longer than what we first thought
So much once again for the weather report!

Gary K Raynes

IN TESCO'S

The bluest eyes beckoned to me
Searching my soul,
Looking for a connection,
They made me stop look and listen.
A woman beside those heavenly eyes
Seemed tortured, contorted, bent out of shape
Remonstrated wildly, cursing out loud
In front of those innocent eyes,
Each word unrecognised, the force
Of the slap changed the expression from
Hurt to despise in a second I saw hate
In those beautiful eyes,
'Don't you embarrass me like that again!'
So harshly spoken to a child whose only
Crime that I could see was that
Wonderful person needed to pee.

George Scott Campbell

MISTY

I hear her cries then shouts of despair
As she kicks out at her garden chair
She lives in a different mixed up world not mine
Doesn't hear the clock chime or ever try to write a rhyme
She never has any spare time

In the morning light she stands alone in her night attire
Looking around her little garden her face blank
Then out comes her watering can full to the brim
Lifting it up high sprinkles water like magic dust
On the grass of green and surrounding soil turning it black
Like thick shining oil

The two hanging baskets get their share of water
A sprinkling in each expecting them to grow
The blooms in shades of red, yellow and blues
Vibrant colours that glow in winter when we have snow
Her flowers made of paper blowing softly now in the summer breeze

To her they must be very real blooms those beautiful paper flowers
As she spends all those morning hours tending her garden with care
Somewhere in that misty mind is a memory that all things need water
In order to survive, to be alive.

Rita V Goodhart

SMOKE

Smoke a lot with you near
Listening to my boring chat
Nothing special, just words
You said I know speech
But I know that lie
Didn't learn a lot but I
Learnt how to write.
Maybe I should learn how
To be more open the way I want
To be, smoking on a roll up that
Took too long to make.

Samantha Morgan

GINGER RULES OK

Night never falls; the sodium street lamps and moon-mirrored solar sheets push back the dark in the perpetual day of the city.

Residents retreat homeward for safety leaving the echoing streets empty for the creatures of the night:

The urbane fox, a nocturnal diner in dustbin delicatessens, patrolling his territory, slips silently through the security railings of the gated community, residents unaware of security breached.

From the shadows he steals an unsuspecting slumbering duck from the water feature's weir, it's neighbours fluttering desperately to flight, escaping an untimely massacre.

Dozing on the sofa, wine sated, patio doors open onto my small jetty, allowing the cool evening breeze in on a sultry summer night . . . I awake.

Assessing the surreal scenario, my eyes meet those of my uninvited visitor. The gaze is held.

Seconds pass. Casually he turns and slinks away, recognising this territory is mine.

Weekend morning sees the much anticipated launch from my jetty;

Maiden voyage of my radio controlled speedboat on the horseshoe water feature.

Carefully placed into water, this beauty gleams, her silver and red reflection a double delight.

With gathering speed she purrs noisily, belying her graceful streamlined form, which skims the water; turning precisely, lapping once, twice . . .

The phone rings; its jarring interrupts my moment of triumph.

The janitor with a red-hot switchboard is calling, reporting the wrath of residents,

I neither know nor see, complaining the boat will scare the ducks.

Reluctantly, my morning maiden ends, allowing the ducks to stay on the menu of this watery restaurant.

Jennifer Rossington

STOP SMOKING

I used to smoke 60 a day
To stop smoking I tried every way
One night I started to chain smoke
I said, 'Mum, take them away. It's no joke.'

The first two weeks were hell
It was really tough truth to tell
After four weeks it wasn't too bad at all
I was determined not to falter or fall

The time came. I had won through
Now my life is brand new
I feel a great weight lifted away
As I look forward to each new day.

Frank Tonner

191

I CALL TO YOU

I call you on the wind, the motion of life
That will blow you to me, as safe as life
As it whispers to you and you come in its invisible grasp
Heading straight towards me, I want it to last
Oh wind, put your arms around and protect her
And don't deny your care
For when I see her I'll see her there
And her hair will be blowing in your care
Oh wind, I call on you

I call to you, the stars glowing at night
To bring her to me so safe and so bright
You'll guide her on the way
It's dark I know
And protect and keep her safe till she's in my glow
But I look up above and you'll know so safely you shine in the impenetrable dark
Keep her safe for me
Keep her safe in your heart
Oh stars, I call on you.

On the day she comes may you be out tonight
And look upon her and treat her right
You're a moon of cause it has to be said
I knew when I looked
It had to be read
You play your part and shine so brightly for her
Oh moon, I call on you.

T McFarlane

TAKEN OVER (LIVING WITH OCD)

You may take a look and say normal isn't me,
But there's something overwhelming which has taken over me
You get on with life, each day bearing something new,
But imagine waking up fearing the thing which powers you.
If you don't complete a task you don't dwell and just move on
But we have to complete and repeat till the urge has gone,
When making a decision the pressure is so strong,
For terrible things will occur if the decision made is wrong.
When time is not alongside you and you are running late,
You still have many tasks to repeat, you know there's no escape.
When in a public place and normality is the key,
Anxiety comes over you, you tap, then tap, then freeze.
When arising in the morning you know what's waiting for you,
For once you lift your head the thing has power over you.
It's you that upsets your family, and you that causes pain,
You feel a total waste of time and your family don't think you're sane.
Living with this life causes so much grief,
You wish your life could be given back
And taken off this thief.
Trapped is what you are, stuck in living a fool.
And they wonder why you'd rather die than continue to live at all.
Every single thing has to be touched so it's just right,
And every step repeated and in every door a slide.
No one understands the frustration that you feel,
They don't have to do it all and still pay the bill.
It's easy to say, just stop it nothing will occur,
But you know what is watching you can make your loved ones hurt.
Every action not done will consequently make you pay,
So there is no chance I am stopping no matter that you say.
To be a normal person and live a normal life,
Is such a wonderful gift to have and should not be taken in your stride.
When living without this pain and powering yourself,
Why you can't all get on, be happy and appreciate your good health.
You don't understand and say normal isn't me,
But I wish you could understand the thing which powers me.
Please don't get annoyed and look deeper in what you see,
Because within all this madness there's a perfect reason to me.

Olivia Ratcliffe

REST

There he lay, the old man,
Supine of body, his fragile mind struggling to remember
Where he was. Or yet, who he was.
He felt, he realised, very tired
But mistily remembered, too,
There had once been a time
He had not felt this way;
Dimly recalling how then
His body had obeyed his every call;
Dimly recalling that once he had been happy.

He fought with what meager mental strength he could command
To remember just when that might have been
And what had made it so.
Slowly, so very slowly, the revelation came:
Ah yes – it was when he had been with Caroline!
His beloved Caroline

He whispered her dear name
A smile shaping his lips as in his mind's eye
He saw her once again.
He yearned, oh how he yearned,
For that time to come once more.

And miraculously, as he did, she came towards him,
Through the mists that gathered in the room.
She smiled at him and said his name
And told him that she loved him;
Gently brushed, with her sweet lips
The smile still sat on his;
And held his hand
And stroked his brow
And said she'd never leave him.

Then swiftly came there two more visitors –
Those brothers, Sleep and Death.
Sleep came first, with gentle stealth,
Tiring yet more his lids,
Smoothing his visage, quietening his breath.

Then stole in Death
Who, judging now the time was ripe,
Joined hands with his brother Sleep
To give the old man their precious gift
Of everlasting rest.
And peace.

G Pash

MY FATHER AT 16

(For my father Ronald Middleton who died of a broken heart 29 June 1923 - 1 June 1987)

You could not really show me
The love you felt inside
Because your mother was cold as ice
She really damaged your pride

So at innocent 16 you went to kill
Any man who stood in your way
Your plane was shot down 3 times in the war
Your life would make a good play

When the fighting died down you had babies
And one of those toddlers was me
But all I ever dreamed for
Was a life of simplicity

My ambition at 16 was to make beautiful clothes
Thank you for 'freedom' I now enjoy
I have the best of everything
Because you suffered so hard as a boy

As for your wife and my mother
On her deathbed she held out her hand
Asked me to find out the truth about life
Then spread kindness all over the land

Father look how creative your daughter is now
See how powerful I have become
I've conquered the world for all it is worth
And in doing so had lots of fun

Kathleen Middleton

THE INVINCIBLE TEAR

A tear as fragile as a wing. As sensitive as a petal.
As mighty as a thorn.
Breaks the bond of two people that for a long time
Have been building walls around their love.
Have been sewing together the strings that kept them together.
Destiny had their fates bound to collide
Bound to ignite as one. Bound for eternity.
But this tear had always been prevented.
Had always been kept in the dark. Until finally
Force could no longer keep it intact.
The soul of the woman had left Mankind.
Had abandoned the years of hard work this
Couple gave to their relationship.
She couldn't have prevented it. Like the prevention
Of her tears. It was bound to happen.
The stars had engraved this in her future.
Without any words of goodbye. Without any
Words of wisdom. Without any words of sorrow
This woman had gone.
The man whose heart had been given to her the
Moment they both met, couldn't feel the loss of
His second half. His missing piece.
The woman had taken his heart with her.
The walls they had been building around their
Love had collapsed. The strings that had been
Sewing them together had been cut. Ripped.
Their relationship had shattered like broken glass.
But this tear. As fragile as a wing. As sensitive as a petal.
As mighty as a thorn.
Had taken hold of this man's weakness and taken control.
This tear that had been kept in the dark
Had finally appeared. Sparked into life.
And there was no holding it back. No preventing.
This man's agony was now controlled by his tears.

Laila Ghossain

THE HORIZON

The days move on
And time has gone
That puts space
Between you and me.

And I must tread
This long, long road
That fate has deemed
My life should be.

I watch the child
That has your face
Leap forward and embrace
Each day with joy.

Young heart and bones
That has no fear
And reaches out with
Everything that I hold dear.

It's then I know
What God has planned
For everyone upon
These lands.

That nothing happens
Quite by chance
He knows! And gives us compensation
In things that make our lives enhanced.

And I know, you are there
Just beyond the far horizon
As you always said you'd be
Waiting, for me!

Joan May Wills

2012

There's much of the royal family on TV
In this twenty-twelve year
Reminding, ever reminding How our Queen is very dear.

William and Kate feature just as much
He's our future king
A good one he'll make too, I feel
Due all sunshine he does bring.

This twenty-twelve is Jubilee year
Of her majesty
With another 60-year-reign
Going down in our history.

Twenty-twelve, too
Occasion's our 'Preston Guild Year'
An every-twenty-years occurrence
If we can find our way clear.

So quite an all-round
Eventful time
When I as a Prestonian
Shall remember twenty-twelve
As being – 'year sublime'.

Barbara Sherlow

WHEN A CITY LOST ITS BREATH

A city lost its heart, a city lost its breath
One sunny day when the world was at rest.
Two strikes of the iron bird in the sky
Into Twin Towers standing so straight, so high.

These twins were the country's backbone of life
But now they have crumbled amid cruel strife.
Fire engine sirens are blasting away
So many lives lost on this fatal day.

But this country's flag has never lost its will to fly
Although many people had seen loved ones die
We live in a world hurting with pain
Please God, I pray it will never happen again.

Margaret Davies

198

LAMENT OF THE SEAL

Oh there you are, I missed you yesterday
I saw you briefly and then you were gone.
Were you watching acrobatic gulls
Or playful ravens tumbling in the sky?
Maybe you were foraging for shells
On craggy beaches washed by salty sea
Did you hear the call of the snipe
Or the eerie sound of oyster catchers?
I called you last night – did you hear me
Or were you deep in your dreamworld?
Will you come again someday
When the wonders of Orkney are seen?

Margaret Lawrance

THE QUARREL

You and me,
mother and daughter,
fire and water.
Depths of unforgiving,
swollen rivers of emotion,
engulfing all before them.
We cannot talk,
we are too alike.
But I love you and miss you.
The sea does not
break on the shore.
The fire does not
warm me.
You in all your
magnificence is
All I desire.

Wendy Gibson

LINES COMPLEX

It starts when you're given that first paper and pen,
For the magic and excitement of life is revealed,
As the ink flows, you watch the first lines appear,
That's now your creation of time, why so thrilled!

Now your line has that magical movement,
For new shapes, of all sorts can be designed.
Ones invented, such as letters and numbers,
The capability of the line now, yours to define!

So now we have lines that tell stories,
Plus the ones full of information and facts.
Then there are those that keep time and count,
Calculating the finances of life, so can't relax!

Then the excitement of lines that come together,
Merging in different colours and forms, wow!
May it be pictures, patterns or simple designs,
Adds to the magic and beauty of lifestyle now!

From notes dancing on lines causing music,
Where one finds sound and emotions blend.
But nature's complex lines set our journey,
Of discoveries and knowledge that will never end!

Ann Beard

THE ICE AGE

In manner insidiously slow, the icy curtain moved across the brooding earth and, in an iron grip the continents held fast.

The world, an infant still, now 'still', is seemed, forever had to be, in timeless sleep, and yet its life but recently begun.

How came it then, that in a space of time the heart's blood that a frozen waste once was, began to flow again?

Had it but lain awhile and, in an awe-full silence, nurtured life, to precociously produce the beauty now beheld for, when the curtain parted once again such majesty there was that the universe had never seen before.

Upon the mountain peaks, residual snow, of sparkling white, gazed back at sister stars, and living things began to grow again, in matchless wonder protesting, yet throbbing with vitality.

Florence Barnard

YOU DON'T UNDERSTAND

I am fox, imagine that . . .
I sneak about to find a place to bask in the sun,
I live at the bottom of a garden,
It seems no one wants me, least of all the cat!
I spend hours at night when no one can see,
Digging a hole to put my young,
I dig over and over again to find it's filled in!
Where shall I go? My house all gone,
Humans just don't understand.
I feel I have rights to trees and pasture land
Tractors have taken this from me –
There's no doubt I'm beautiful and will do you no harm,
Give me a chance to bask in the sun,
My life is hard so little to eat,
You don't understand,
I want a little space, a little land to call my own,
I'll do you no harm.
I've grown very timid, my rations are low,
I grow very thin, my face I hardly show.
I'm hiding now, waiting for a chance to roam,
Survive, and bask in the sun,
In a secret place that no one knows,
I venture out once more, I'm behind your tree,
But you cannot see me,
Take pity, have you any scraps for me?
Perhaps *you* understand?

Liz Dicken

THE JUBILEE AND ME

What a year 2012 has been
A reign of sixty years for our Queen
I have celebrated less publicly
Eighty years old, good enough for me.

The Queen had parties of all manner
A long wet cruise upon a river
My treat a little more mundane
A ride upon a Harley Davidson!

Her majesty and I both delighted
With family and friends all united
None the less we all agreed
A milestone reached so gloriously.

Forget the bunting and decorations
We both enjoyed our celebrations
Royal and historical I may not be – but
For just one day, equality for her majesty and me.

Freda Symonds

THE WISE FOOL

A man who can sing
When he hasn't got a thing
Is either a fool;
Or can outrank a king.
A man who helps those,
Deserving in need.
With no thought for himself;
And oblivious to greed.
Stands out from the crowd,
And his silence is loud.
Be him fool;
Or thought odd.
He's known to his god.

Windsor Hopkins

THE SEASONS OF AGE

Spring is when we are born
And learn to live and grow
Welling up from the seed
The leaves begin to show
Summer is our active years
When we're busy all the time
The plant grows strong and healthy
And really looks just fine.
Autumn brings maturity
When wisdom comes along
The flowers are at their best
Perfection does belong.
Then winter bring its problems
With disability and poor health
But no one can take away
The wisdom that is wealth.
Just because we're older
We still can have real life
Whatever our situation
Even if we're in strife.
The nuggets from our younger lives
Still can shine through
Helping those in trouble
Like caring people do.
We may not rush around so much
But we have a lot to give
For all that we've experience
Can really help others live.
We still have our talents
Which flower like can shine
So take advantage of them
Your need combined with mine.
Old age is not easy
But if we use it well
It really can inspire the young
If only we will tell.

Rita Hardiman

COMING HOME

When you were wee you had a dream
A dream that then came true.
Your future you had planned with care
You worked and studied to get there.

You looked so smart as you marched by,
Saluting your country's flag.
I was so proud of my soldier son.
Though my life of worry had just begun.

Your words that day as you flew away
You joked, to sunnier climes –
You kissed and hugged me and gave me a smile
'Don't worry Love, I'll be fine.'

And while you worked at your dream job,
I kept busy to make time pass by.
Never watching the news, as they broadcast the score.
Always dreading that knock on my door.

Your precious words lived within my heart
Till the day I stood on the tarmac and watched
With bated breath, and tears that flowed.
The plane came down – the ramp was lowered
You walked into my arms – you smiled
And whispered – 'I told you so.'

Pat Kennedy

A ROYAL JUBILEE

A thousand ships in from the sea
We celebrate our Queen's Jubilee
The pop show with a special cast
Over our head was a magic flypast
Our special family on a royal balcony
We help to plant a Jubilee tree
A flame upon a countryside hill
At Westminster we all had a fill
March behind a royal army band
See folk here from every far-off land.

A special service at dear St Paul's
The street party in every council halls
Lights upon the royal palace side
From the rain, poor people they hide
News from over the entire world
Four days of holidays we held
Carriages drive along The Mall
Ships by engines and then by sail
On the throne for sixty years
Bring our normal folk to tears.

The church bells they start to chime
Never again in our own lifetime
Tower Bridge they start to raise
Aircraft fly from out a haze
Sixty years upon the British throne
Queen Elizabeth spent days alone
Folk they came by air and sea
The Queen there with her family
Words of joy and words of love
Our Queen with prayers from above.

Colin Allsop

THE HURRICANE

The hurricane caught us unaware,
And now everything has been left bare,
Houses and lives been lost by the score,
People killed but not by war,
Our young Jim was out playing that day
The hurricane has blown him and others away,

They have been blown far out to sea,
Just like all the other debris,
My wife, she cries her tears of woe,
But her grief she must show,
Our little boy was only three,
And now he's in Heaven, an angel to be,

Who is to blame for this tragic fate?
Even now, after it's too late,
The weathermen say they did not know,
About the tragic hurricane show,
Now all of us and friends as well,
Are left with nothing at all to sell,

We are bereft of our little boy who
Brought us all such wonderful joy,
He has gone in the hurricane's wake,
As well as all the other people it did take,
So all we have now are memories
Of our little boy whose smile brought
Us so much joy, just
A photo in a frame but we will never
Forget his name.

Roy Muir

THE EQUILIBRIUM OF FRIENDSHIP

Friendship is like the smell of scrambled eggs on toast.
Friendship is like the possession of things you desire most.
Friendship is like the warming of toes, when you are cold.
Friendship is like the sight of a baby, one minute old.
Friendship is like a special tenderness.
Friendship is like an annual bonus, no less.
Friendship is like the aroma of freshly baked bread.
Friendship is like the beauty of sunsets of red.
Friendship is like a stretched out hand when you fall.
Friendship is like the strength of a solid brick wall.
Friendship is like a breath of clean fresh air.
So try to offer friendship to all everywhere.
To my friends, I wish everything that is the best.
To my enemies, I just wish to say, 'God bless.'

Yvonne Chapman

BODY

The sea choppy and uninviting
Under a gloomy sky.
An ill and sleety wind blows constantly.

Her shroud, shreds of ochre kelp
Entwine her nakedness.
Resting in the creamy sand
Laundered by the sea.

A red, dead starfish lies beside her,
For company.

Body swollen,
Eyes glassy and doll-like.
Face of china clay,
Still beautiful even in death.
Skin assaulted by scavenging gulls.
Legs splayed obscenely,
Unnatural pose.
Clothes flung and scattered around her,
Sodden!

In the distance,
A black, private ambulance approaches
To retrieve her sad and sombre body.

Roy Goucher

ALMOST KEEPING UP APPEARANCES

They say many a true word is spoken in jest,
Usually by Onslow, when dressed in his vest.
Daddy is listening with vacant expression,
Whilst Violet suffers her normal depression.
Her husband has started cross-dressing again,
Causing her heart a great deal of pain.
Hyacinth's busy arranging her suppers,
Whilst Richard is busy unblocking the gutters.
He who hesitates is lost,
As Richard well knows to his cost.
Elizabeth continues spilling her coffee,
Elevenses with Hyacinth, cloying as toffee.
Emmet is hiding, keeping at bay,
Far out of Hyacinth's way he must stay.
He wants to avoid her and her suppers,
Her thoughts of musical evenings scuppered.
Hyacinth rushes to the phone,
More haste, less speed, if truth be known.
Perhaps it's Sheridan, her son,
Boy wonder, not to be outdone.
She doesn't know that he is gay,
And keeping well out of her way.
He only telephones for cash,
And always tells her, he must dash.
As Hyacinth seeks to improve her station,
By determined social elevation.
Gather ye rosebuds whilst ye can,
For time and tide, wait for no man.
Daisy needs Onslow for good times all round,
As Onslow watching the racing is found.
He only watches it on the telly,
His string vest turning Daisy to jelly.
She imagines riding in his car,
Thoughts of romance never far.
A trip to the woods would be the ticket,
For a bit of a cuddle in the thicket.
A bird in the hand is worth two in the bush,
And the greenery does look temptingly lush.

Young Rose is on the prowl again,
Not many chances now remain.
A fool and his money are soon to be parted,
If Rose's new beau is not faint-hearted.
They all seem content, though goodness knows why,
It's better to always let sleeping dogs lie.

Jacqueline Burns

UK'S DILEMMA

The world's gone mad.
Clearing forests to grow
More fuel, environmentally
Friendly they say.
Killing all little animals
Depriving them of their homes.

Local building on
Green field sites or
Right in the middle of the town
Creating more traffic
Chaos and pollution
And the need for more fuel.

This roundabout of destruction
Goes on and on
Local government has to look
To London for directives and budgets
Our government has to obey
The European directive
Where's the sense?
Where's the logic?
What does the Eu
Know about UK Post Offices?

Elizabeth T Jenks

FREEDOM

Today I have time. It was not always so
Being disabled does have its constraints
Both for carer as well as the patient
Restricted by tablets, doctors, wheelchairs and ramps
Was there resentment at these limitations?
Not at the time, love softened the blow.

Now I have time to spend as I wish,
Selfish, or not, the freedom is welcome.
Going to bed at the time of my choice
Eating those foods of personal preference.
Staying out late; going home in the dark
Travelling the world and making new friends
Meeting and sharing with those from the past
These ongoing pleasures, one's joy is complete.

Di Hinves

EARTHLING

What am I but a little bit of earth;
Part of the planet of that very name,
Which wrought me, nurtured me and gave me birth.
Yet ev'n this matrix earth that I may claim
My own, was born herself within the bosom
Of an earlier, mothering, grand dame.
The archive cosmos bears the dust clues
To that great family tree, whose scion-star
The sun, was seeded by another, sarabanding
Round the great galactic girth,
Where I was but a little bit of earth.

Walter Blacklaw

MANGETOUTS

Tell me, oh tell me
Why people do
Go really potty
Over a mangetout?

What is its secret?
I fail to see
My friends go crazy
And have them for tea

You needn't be clever
Or have a degree
To recognise the fact
It's only a pea.

Sandra Noyes

COLOUR BLUE

I do not know why I am sad
But an old memory haunts me
Of many, many years ago
When as waiting at Chelmsford station
I saw a young woman on the platform opposite
Wearing a blue dress

Then a train pulled in and she was gone
Just a glimpse, no more

Yet since then not a week has passed
When I don't think of
The woman wearing a blue dress.

Kevin Cobley

THE UNKNOWN ONE

They sit closeted in their ivory tower
The faceless ones who make the laws.
Their minions, like sheep, gather around in the fold
But we will never know the first person who
Mutes an idea in the sheep pen.
When the big chief says, 'I've got an idea'
The sheep all, 'Baa!' with one accord.
The chief is very pleased with such a flock.
One day he said, 'We will make a bomb'
They all nodded in unison.
The bomb was made and kept in store
In case the wolf-enemy should venture near,
Thus they had the power to rule the world, these
Faceless ones who make the laws . . .
Came the day when storm clouds gathered
Around the sheep in the ivory towers,
The enemy was drawing near and unease was among the flock.
Nothing daunted, the boss man said, 'Do not fear
We have the bomb, we can defeat our enemies.'
The sheep were calmed, the big chief sighed.
'First I need a volunteer to press the red button.'
His minions, with eyes downcast, moved not a muscle
And spoke not a word . . .

Doreen Gardner

THE TRUTH SHALL SURFACE

When diamond stars were burning bright at night
When brilliant sunlight evaporated inky darkness away
There we were, proud people witnessing a new day
And there you were, devising a deviously dangerous game.

No good moaning or groaning if a secret is revealed
It was you who busily conspired on purpose against me
It was not you who knew how my injuries healed
It was me who swam through the sea of tragedy
It was I who finally finished the race to victory.

What were my thoughts when you called me your friend?
Over the years your sincerity shrunk in true value
On all occasions my friendship you pretend to defend
Why you cheated on me, what now must I expect
For the structural damage is done but will it mend?
No, there were signals when this friendship was wrecked.

The truth shall surface, often its message is of surprise
The truth shall surface and scupper our dreadful lies
So when seemingly there's no glimmer of hope in hell
Courage on the day and honesty together will tell
For justice is our guide, do remember it with pride.

John Flanagan

GAZELLE OF TRANQUILITY

'The dead learn nothing by heart – but gratitude.' Jane Austen

What we see in your books of sand is the past,
The far past that is a realm of dust and gold.
Who are you? We ask; and get no answer but misty fields.
Who are you? We pass on a street leading us nowhere.
In your hazel eyes love was in disarray like uncombed hair,
At daybreak when one rises from an uneven night's sleep.
And yet your name has been carved on a pomegranate fruit
In the garden of dusk, for you have placed your dream
Landscapes like flowering jasmine in our open hands, as a gift.
We see you as luminescent – without boundaries –
As when, you polished the silver cups of daybreak.
Must we go on opposite paths in separate directions?
Here though you have left us only the breadcrumbs of departure;
Are we not two shadows becoming one, opening and shutting like a fan?
Look, there is one land bordering another within me now,
Filled, both, with your oval eyes and the crystal night of your absence.
Look, there is no language for what life could be – but yours.
Tell me, luminous moon will rise also in my dark night?
Exiled in death are you now neither nostalgia nor promise?
How *are* you now on the other side – the same or different?
Though far from the moon are you worn smooth by moonstones?
Walking among the dead do you learn nothing by heart – but gratitude?
Look! If you will I'd rest your shadow against that elm tree,
Turn rusted iron and ruins for you into moonlight;
For you are no shallow river full of ambiguous pebbles.
Maybe you journey on alternately in light and darkness,
As we do, left behind on Earth looking back on you;
Perhaps your journeying heart still reaches a harbour;
Or comes on a door behind which are fragrant gardens.
Do you remember anything still that's earth-side?
Transparent, tranquil meadows – a raging storm among trees?
I see Blake sitting with Cowper next to you smiling;
'One day we will be what we want to be,' you say.
Is your wound now a star, an amphora, a fountain?
A stairway to gentler times now time for you is no more?
Open your door to my poem if you want to do so.
Look! Everyone dies and few are remembered on dying;
But no one is utterly dead who died as you did

With friends who loved her; and you have now on Earth
Many brothers and sisters and fathers and mothers
Who love you because of the virgin beauty of your fine prose,
And smile at your sly irony. They're now family.
Another heaven on Earth – like the one above us.

Alan C Brown

JUST THINKING

Legs swinging, I sit on a seat in the sun
Nearby, on the beach, holiday families have fun
They're laughing and shouting and all full of glee
Enjoying their freedom, down by the sea.

A little way inland. Stands a nursing home,
Where life now goes on slowly, especially for some
No longer following a normal routine
Entirely relying on time that has been
Their world now encompassed in well-padded cots
Now sleeping, now waking, not caring two jots
For the noise and frenzy of the outside world
Their banners of life once so bravely unfurled
Now frayed out and tattered, ready to drop
Life's breath so fragile now, could suddenly stop.

The tide comes in, the tide goes out.
Nobody knows what it's all about.

Vera Sykes

MODERN LIFE

Computers rule us every day
We must conform to what they say!
But when the systems all go down
There's pandemonium on the ground.

Mobile phones are glued to ears
So conversation disappears
It's texting, texting, all the way
Whilst music on the iPads plays.

The modern youth, they learn so fast
And leave us 'old ones' out of grasp
Technology has left behind
That *human element* of Mankind.

Heather Overfield

GLANYFERRI

O to be in Ferryside
Now that April's here.
Gazing over the shimmering sleeve
Of sea-river, or river-sea
Towards distant Llansteffan
With its ancient castle
Like Camelot.
A broken necklace
Adorning the headland
But forever in danger
Of slipping into the sea.
Low down on the hill,
Below the toppling terraces
The toy train rattles along
Beside the shore.
And out on the gleaming water
Yachts spin this way and that
Like mayflies in a dance.
I pace out the beach
Between the groynes
Captain of all I survey
On a wild, sunny April day.

Mari Dafis

CIRCLE OF LIFE

Lost in a dream, we see pictures,
Pictures of days gone by.
Seeing the memories unfolding
Our minds gently look back and sigh.
Remembering school days with pleasure
Although time dims pain, it is clear
The friends that we made in our learning years
Are the ones we hold most dear.
Suddenly one is grown up,
At least that is thought at the time.
But life has a habit of turning sour
Just when you feel all is fine.
Pain hits us all somewhere, somehow
But experience and love show us the way
To go forward and deal with adversity
And resolve any problem day by day.
Relationships gather momentum
And for some marriage fills a void.
And a family is born in a tide of love
The next generation to guide.
Growing old is part of a pattern,
And death comes to us all in the end.
With despair at the losing there is joy in the gaining
And the circle of life starts again.

Elizabeth Timmins

UNTITLED

You left me too early, you shouldn't have gone
We had so much to share and so much to say,
Our time was so precious, then stole away.

Are you looking down, watching over me? And if you are what do you see?
Are you wondering where the year has gone, or are you still with me, and I have it wrong?

Many times I hoped you would appear – mistaken identity and a wasted year.
But when I awake from a fretful sleep, I realise the truth, turn over and weep.

I should let your spirit run over ocean and sea, perhaps my pain would subside
And I could survive.

Janice Melmoth

TELL ME WHAT YOU HEAR

I'm listening intently, won't you share my joy –
A gentle breeze blowing, the birds in full song.
A walk in the countryside, sun shining bright.
A tiny lamb bleating fills me with delight.
A tractor turns furrows, the soil rich and red.
The noise is vibrating – the hard work goes on.
There's interest and promise with seeds in the ground,
The insects are buzzing, there's life all around.
I want you to listen, with hope in your heart,
All worries are smothered, the sun is quite warm.
The river flows softly and soothes every care,
The peace of the countryside we can all share.
A skylark sings sweetly high up in the sky,
Some young rabbits scamper as I pass close by.
A hawk's raucous call as she too flies high,
I make my way homeward as evening draws nigh.
The church bells are ringing, there's hope in the sound,
We savour their music and find peace of mind.
There's much in this world, and we all play a part,
By listening we learn – and there's joy in our hearts.

Glenys B Moses

EMOTIONS

Emotion is a sensation weaving in one's mind,
Ticking daily but we are unaware of it most of the time,
Emotion can reach many levels of lows and highs,
Emotion can mean passion, love, desire and elations,
Emotions come from the heart stirred by motivations,
Emotions can be felt by parental or siblings' instinct,
Emotion can break a heart or make it soar in an instant,
Emotions can be very dangerous if fuelled by hate,
Emotions are thoughts, wishes, hopes and fears hard to sedate,
Emotions can also bring us great warm feelings of joy,
A hug from a child, someone saying I love you.
A little baby's first smile, are just a few of the happy emotions,
Which make this emotional life all the more worthwhile.

Elizabeth Moore

218

THE DOLL

It was the 25th December, they call it Christmas Day
That's when we got some chocolate and toys with which to play
I was so filled with excitement I ran barefoot to the hall
Then took the stairs at such a pace, not frightened of a fall

I saw the bulging stocking, an orange in the toe
A bright pink box sat next to it, what it held I did not know
I opened up my present to see what had been bought
I was a little older then, Santa wasn't in my thought

A rose bud doll looked up at me from her little cardboard nest
Of all the things I'd ever had, this simply was the best
I carried her around with me until after our big lunch
Then I had to go out with my Mam to visit Lizzie French

I was not allowed to take my doll, my brothers stayed with Dad
Because they could not be trusted and often were quite bad
When I arrived back home that day my doll could not be found
The only thing that I could see, were two cowboys on the ground

They pleaded they were innocent with sly looks upon their face
Then scurried down the passage to a secret hiding place
I quickly hurried after them and they told me such a tale
Of little wailing banshees that had taken my doll away

They said she'd had her hair cut off and been given evil spells
And if I ever looked at her I would surely go to Hell
The fear was in my bloodstream, it gripped me like a vice
As I lay in my bed that night not turning off the light

Then I heard a scraping, outside my bedroom door
Next there was a tapping on the upstairs landing floor
I lay there in a panic and really had to wee
When the door burst open, a whimper came from me

There was a thud next to be bed and I looked down just to see
My doll that had no eyes or hair was staring up at me
The screams that left my body could be heard in Timbuktu
And with the speed I left my bed it felt like I flew

As I ran to seek the refuge of my mother's loving arms
I didn't see the giggling boys behind the potted palms.

Elizabeth Dey

MUSIC ON THE WING

Why this unattended birdbath pool
Must be water shortage conservation rule
Seems once storms raged
Rain gushed from sky
Now raindrops few, reservoirs
And our pool runs dry.

For elderly people hosepipe ban
Just to let you know
Zimmer frames, walking aids have you
Not noticed, heavy watering can on duty
One's progress going slow
Garden plants struggle
All living things that thirst
Waiting elusive phenomenal wonder
A cloud burst

Do not fret, breakfast time as usual
No ban yet, could not bear to miss
The squabble scraps on lawn
Liquidised leftover dips, bathtime fun
You relished, pool now empty, dejected
No visitors unloved forlorn.

Soon one hopes rain resumed refreshment
Sprinklers smile, no doubt new grumbles come
By nature sun loves glum, to be compatible
Friendly as the birds that call, each day
Amusing, regardless of the weather, cheerful
Uncomplicated style, harmony
In chorus together sing
Dawn till late our pleasure, their gift
'Music on the wing'.

Mildred Barney

ROCHESTER CASTLE

Early morning mists swirl around the castle's keep
Rochester's ancient castle in history is steeped.
It stands proud on the shore of the River Medway,
Many warring armies in it did stay.

In the past it was of great import,
Great battles for its control have been fought.
Now it stands majestic and battle weary,
Scarred and battered by war's fury.

Today 'Friends of the Castle' show visitors around,
The views from the battlements will astound.
The green downs, woods and fields are for all to see,
The River Medway adds to a picture of beauty you will agree.

The castle grounds each year are home to many a celebration,
It is directly attached to the famous Rochester High St
For visitors making it a desirable combination.
The 'Charles Dickens' and the 'Sweeps' festivals keep Rochester's history alive,
Oldie world presentations help to make the Medway towns thrive.

On a summer's evening sitting by the Medway's river side,
One can vision knights and soldiers in their stride,
Preparing for battle, to defeat the oncoming foe,
Fighting hand to hand, blow to blow.

You are glad you are in Rochester today,
Missing the blood and gore of another affray.
Go home tonight and enjoy your sleep,
Let the past of Rochester historians keep.

Terry Godwin

CONFETTI

Little bits of paper,
Flying in the air.
Brightly coloured wishes,
Floating everywhere.
Different shapes of blessings,
Tossed in joyful waves.
Some all bright and sparkly,
The couple's steps will pave.
These tiny papered rainbow dots,
Have a motion all their own,
And manage to get into spots,
Where clothes are firmly sewn.
Into your hair, they boldly stick,
And on your face they land.
To throw and run's the clever trick,
But it's never as you planned.
Excitement grows, as bride appears,
And the confetti's into play.
It's a custom, echoing the years,
And makes this special day.
Wedding's done, and home you go,
This nuisance shower rains down.
As you bustle to and fro,
In your dressing gown.
You find it in the bathroom,
And on the bedroom floor.
The pieces at you, start to loom,
To remove them is a chore.
In USA confetti's out,
They reverently throw rice.
But waves of this, can give a clout,
Use confetti's my advice.
The only good thing in their ploy,
Is the fact they don't clear up.
The birds are waiting every day,
These morsels for to sup.
But rice has no expression,
No colour, shapes or fun.
Confetti's the exception,
It's loved by everyone.
Held in little paper bags,
By the joyful throng.
This simple custom, never flags,
And helps the day along.

222

When asked to a wedding grand,
Join the merry waiting fray.
Then hold confetti, tight in hand,
Throw and run away.

Duchess Newman

MARRIAGE

Life teaches but first it taught
That marriage is great and not so tough
However the experience I faced
Was a tragic mistake
They complained and complained but never gave
Today we don't heed to advice
Tomorrow we will be the victims of lies
This pain I shed, this pain I express
Look carefully and do not make the same regrets
Be grateful because of the advice you've got
We always forget but never forgot
I scream aloud to warn you now
To follow my advice as it is profound
The pain I carried, oh God help us
The pain I experienced, it was grief.
Now they listen, at first they never believed
I cried and cried until my eyes went blind
The quiet voices I carried are what they finally find
The pain I tell, the pain I told
Only I experienced this, no one could ever know
This pain I tell, this pain I told
Listen to my advice or you will never know.

Saira Anwar

223

BRIEF ENCOUNTER

I noticed her among the summer fruits,
Freshness and shapeliness her attributes.
She led me down a strangely quite aisle
And met someone she knew – oh what a smile!
Together we ploughed on through vegetables
And seemed agreed on waiving cereals
But then we parted ways, she to the bread
While I indulged in alcohol instead.
I feared I'd savour bitters on my own
And have no use for seed, my bird now flown.
I sadly mourned my loss with flowers and very
Soon took comfort in confectionery
But glimpsed her at the delicatessen
From pharmacy and a medical lesson.
My hope was raised and – she was there!
Lovely as a vision in underwear.
I lost my zest for manager's reductions
With thoughts all turned to possible seduction.
Past frozen meat I felt myself much bolder
But all that I received was her cold shoulder.
Despite that, I moved close to check her out;
She turned on me with such a dreadful shout:
'Creep! Are you off your trolley? Basket case!'
I fled the supermarket in disgrace.

Michael Robertson

THREE CHARMS

Bullying and violence and murder,
News of these too often hits the viewer –
Actions that enfeeble much our nation,
Which now spends a lot on education.

School from four to sixteen moulds the many –
Others' growth in poise is hardly any.
Messages of kindness fail to get there,
Barred by moods of social don't-know don't-care.

Youth for whom all peace is just too peaceful,
Who find eating, drinking, both too easeful,
Get on others' nerves to soothe their boredom,
Seeing self as vital to escape from.

Education, training or employment
Are three charms that can restore enjoyment.
Only minds that focus on construction
Block the timeless hazards of destruction.

Time to quit those 'overrated pleasures'.
Bring on all the 'underrated treasures'.
That old song that warned of tricky waters
Cries for heeding in so many quarters.

Allan Bula

IN THIS CHURCH

Between my thoughts
Were childhood statues
Returning expressions
Of frozen meanings
Where I was alone
With relics breathing souls
Of Constantia and Felix
Remembering Sundays in church
With pulpit inspirations
From Father Karol's
Arrangements for life
And settled bereavements.
I journeyed back
To the tired stations
Forever hanging to the cause
To colourful stories unfolding
From reading of stained glass
Chapters in my space
Silent corner for Mary
Of family preference
Cosy side altar bay
And wooden panel nets
For nativity windows
Of enchantment,
Replay of the organ
To yesterday's voices
From choir balcony hideaway
But dark solemn place
Where servers we were
From memory steps
And bells chiming softer
Congregations in same places
Touching echoes
In hazy conclusions
Where walls spoke a haven for peace.
When candles were shortening
Down in an old baptistery
Was another reminder
As the church continued to whisper
In yesterday.

Richard Leduchowicz

SISTERS

Dear Martha, how very much I love her,
And how in her own strange way
She loves me.

Dear Martha, always so very busy
With active, energetic love,
Always doing things.

Dear Martha, how much I ache for her,
And wish sometimes she
Could simply relax.

Dear Martha, only her way is right:
Even the master came in for his share
Of criticism from her.

Dear Martha, fussing about the dinner
And what to put before our famous guest;
How she complained of me.

Dear Martha, how angry she was
When the master told her not to worry so,
But come and join me.

Dear Martha, she could not see
That he wanted to talk and be with us,
And not to eat.

Dear Martha, why does she not realise
That she had the chance to know him,
And was too preoccupied?

Dear Martha, why is it that I always sigh
Whenever I make mention of her
And speak her name?

Robert Toogood

UNSUNG HEROES

There have been many unsung heroes
The gungadins of this world
Water carriers, carrying the can amidst foes
Thus life-long friends, evolved and unfurled

Harry Secombe, Spike Milligan, Peter Sellars
John Cleese, Michael Bentine, Tommy Cooper,
Benny Hill, Dick Emery all funny fellas
Clive Dunne, Bud Flanegan a veteran trooper

The First World War before my time
All's quiet on the Western front!
Boy soldiers, killed before their prime
Missed their siblings' baptism in the font

The lady of the lamp, Florence Nightingale
Her shadow the wounded didst kiss
Called, so was bound to prevail
Fruitless obstacles, she wouldst dismiss.

Jennifer Margaret Hudson

FAITH IN THE FUTURE

From this day forward, a new century has begun
And new worlds and nations, should rise as one
In this new time what will the future hold for
Those of us who are now growing old?
Have those who took the burden the strength to hold?

In this new age, where shall they start?
Now taking a giant step into the dark

Trust in our fellow man, have faith in their abilities
Hearing what they have to say and listening to their views
Every nation shall speak peace into its neighbour

Faith in the future is what we all need
Unblocking their minds of those who want to lead
Teaching the children to have love and respect
Urging them to learn in this brand new world
Reaching out, searching out, looking far beyond
Ensuring the world will be an Eden to the end.

Shirley-Patricia Cowan

ONE OF THE FAMILY

See him sleep the old dog
As he lies by the fire.
Snorts and twitches in dreams
Of young canine desire.
He could outrun the fleetest
And out-bark the best,
That elastic small bundle of mischief and zest.
Sleek and shining his coat,
Bright and sparkling his eyes
Vibrating with health and fun,
. . . We realise
He ignored most commands –
Had his way in the end.
He was spoiled, and we spoiled him –
He is man's best friend.
Now, old age is upon him –
Dull of coat, blind of eye.
Stiff-jointed – confused, but he's still game to try.
He still barks at strangers –protecting his own.
Still hears a loud voice, a doorbell, a phone
Still follows his master and sits by his chair
And we love him and need him and worry and care
We dread thoughts of parting – when he won't be there
With his welcoming bark and his wag of the tail
Uncomplaining, uncritical, faithful and frail.
But I know in my heart we shall meet him again
Sharing his doggy dreams – full of joy – free of pain.
For such trust and devotion must last for all time.
All old friends reunited . . .
That dream is mine.

Edna Mills

OPERATION BELLY

I'm a happy person most of the time, that's true,
But something happened out of the blue.
I had an op, hernia on my belly.
As it gave me gip and a lot of welly.
So they had to do a repair,
Had it done without a care.
A week later I was back in,
It became infected, the horrid thing.
Opened up and made it all okay,
20 clips down my belly had to stay.
A week later, ouch, they came out,
I was quiet good, but did I shout.
A week later it was passing bad,
Again to the hospital, I was sad.
Opened up again, to remove the slime,
All in all it was the fifth time.
Battered and bruised and very sore,
The stitches came out and I prayed, no more.
It's been a week
So far it's fine,
No more ops!
That belly's mine.
So I've had my fill and I'd like to say.
Today's the day, I'm having a good day!

Stephanie Lynn Teasdale

THE GHOST WHO ONCE LOVED YOU

Will you miss me when I'm dead?
When all the crap has been misread?
The music could play a silent tune.
Like dust blowing under a timeless moon.
Would you pretend you cared when I was alive?
Saying you wished I was well and did survive.
How you loved my company, how we were friends,
I could not see.
Will you miss me when I am gone?
Say a few hypocritical words at the podium.
Pretend and make out you knew me at all,
Said hello, made one single telephone call.
I watch you at my hearse side
Crying and wishing I had not died
I haunt you because I loved you in life
Wishing we had made it to husband and wife.
Am I real live time misread?
As a phantom I'm with you, oh so much I could have said!
As my coffin is lowered, do I see a tear fall?
As the will is read, I will come through the wall.
I face the morning, I'm at the end of your bed.
Will you miss me when I'm dead?

Barry Powell

CHERISH THE LOVE YOU HAVE

We should cherish the time we have together
For little do we know when it will cease
When trouble and calamity break out
We should enter the Lord's peace

Do not take each other for granted
But with praise and gratitude
To love, honour and adore
That should be the attitude

Be always there for one another
Whatever comes you way
Greet each other with a kiss and a smile
At the start of each new day

Learn to bear with one another
Even with the things that irritate
For when you can love each other that way
That's the start of something great

Look out for one another
Bring little pleasures of joy
Be it through a flower or card
Or even a cuddly toy

When you learn the secret of loving
From the bottom of your heart
Help to nurture and let it flourish
And from it never depart

Make your mark upon this world
So when you go to God in glory
Others who remember you
Will always have a story.

Jean Hazell

A RAINBOW OF DREAMS
(For my children)

After the storm, as peace ascended
Over the hillsides, upon the furrowed land –
Then appeared, in a silence transcended,
A beauteous array as though by God's hand,
Shimmering in the distance, a wondrous sight
Above the dripping greenery of the trees –
A magical glimpse thro' rays of sunlight,
Disappearing far away among the leas,
My rainbow of dreams – and schemes.

And as I gazed at the deep brown soil,
Where once we had rested by farmer's gate,
In contemplation of so much hard toil
Sheltered, waiting for the storm to abate,
We fed our eyes on the fresh green wheat
We knew would reach its promised state –
And church-bells rang out a steady beat,
Summoning the harvest, God's hand to await.
Aided by my rainbow of dreams.

Then, as those bright colours faded away,
Birds sang sweetly – to end another day –
And gentle harmony reigned anew.

Julia Eva Yeardye

THE HOMELESS

How can we sleep so sound in our beds,
Knowing so many folks have no roof over their heads,
Making shacks out of newspaper and cardboard boxes,
Looking for food in waste bins like the foxes?

They can't get jobs as they have no fixed address,
No wonder their lives are in such a mess,
They wait for many days to get money from the state
So they sit and beg for money to be thrown on a plate,

Don't judge these people because they have to roam
It's certain circumstances that mean they have lost their home,
So when you see them beg, there's no option for them to take,
It's the only way to buy a cup of tea and a piece of cake,

If they're lucky for one night they have a free bed,
Charitable people making sure they are fed,
But it doesn't last long, it soon comes to an end,
It's out on the streets again themselves to depend,

In this day and age it just doesn't seem right,
That people are living in such a terrible plight,
If it was a tropical island, it wouldn't be so bad,
But here in damp cold England it is really very sad,

So when you're feeling warm and snug in your cosy bed,
Just give a thought of what I have said,
These people are human like you and I,
If they're out in the cold too long they will die.

Pauline Xena

IT'S NEVER TOO LATE

'It's never too late,' the landlord said,
As he raised his poor tenant's rent.
'It's never too late to admit your sins,
And show that you really repent.'

'It's never too late,' the loan shark said,
As he knocked on his debtor's door.
'It's never too late to explain your ways
And show how you're actually helping the poor.'

'It's never too late,' the financier said,
As he spent someone else's savings.
'It's never too late to amend your ways,
And make an excuse for your greed and your cravings.'

'It's never too late,' the pornographer said,
As he floated his filth on the net.
'It's never too late to justify porn,
And to grab all the dosh you can get.'

'It's never too late,' the arms dealer said,
'To trade with the rifle and pistol,
To show how each morning you get out of bed
With a conscience as clear as a crystal.'

It's never too late, the five of them thought,
As they stood on that day at the end of time,
To explain the effects of their lives and their work
And show how their efforts had aided Mankind.

But the judge disagreed, and their sentence was harsh;
They whined and protested, 'We just didn't know!
We thought we had plenty of time to be good!
And now it's too late, so – which way do we go?'

Ken Brown

THE RECKONING

Most wondrous God in all of time
Before you we will stand
Stripped naked of all human things
When time runs out of sand.

Like Adam we will stand in shame
Undressed of all our pride
Our wrongs laid out before you
None can be put aside.

Lord you took on the suffering
That we should bear through sin
So every loving Christian
Is cleansed of guilt within.

Let all the world bow down in shame
For things they cannot see
Without the love of Jesus Christ
Who knows where we would be.

And when we stand before you
Great loving God of mine
Don't let us merely hang our heads
Not remembering our crime.

If only for a second
Let us feel what you went through
It's the least we can expect Lord
Through you we're now brand new.

Alma Taylor

MEMORIES

Where shall I store my memories? . . . Elusive things they are.
Slipping through my fingers at the slightest touch.
Things long gone but fresh and sweet as new baked bread.
Thoughts, scents, sounds, glimpses of lost childhood.
Where shall I keep them for safety?
On a high shelf out of reach from prying eyes?
No. They are to be kept dust free and accessible.

I see a small girl crying for Mummy . . .
The world is too big – too frightening . . .
This grown-up world of school.

I smell Sunday teatime dripping toast,
Feel scorched cheeks, while glowing coals turn soft while slices
Into crisp brownness at the end of the toasting fork.

I hear the North Sea sucking at sand
As wavelets tickle toes,
And smell of donkey as I clutch his rough hair,
Scared of falling.

Where shall I keep them – these precious memories?
Put them on computer disc perhaps?
No – they may get wiped away,
I must never lose them – no, not even the sad ones,
I have discarded grief but poignant memories must remain to be re-lived at will.

I see the bride and smell the rose bouquet,
Observe the hastily wiped tear, the groom's proud smile.
I hear baby cries and infant laughter.
Family squabbles, family outings, family Christmas.
Family at the heat of it all.

Yes, the heart – That's where I'll store them . . . locked deep where no one can steal.
And there they'll stay inviolate,
Until, at my last breath they are released with my soul
To go winging into eternity. The laughs . . . the tears . . . the fun . . . the life –
My life.

Kath Hurley

PRAYER AND WORSHIP

Lord use me every day
And hear me while I pray
For people who are lost
You paid the cruel cost
Lord I love you so
I want you to know
You're my everything
Jesus, Lord, my King
I praise Your holy name always
I pray for children in the desert
I pray for children in the street
I pray for people who are hurting
Will You meet their every need?
I bring you families
Oh listen to my pleas
May they be forgiven
And find a place in Heaven
You're my all in all
At Your feet I fall
In humble adoration
With joy and jubilation
I will follow You all my days
I will follow You all my days.

Issy Donaldson

JACK'S UNION

His face was all painted in red, white and blue,
His hands were all willing to help at the do,
Jack's flags were all out and flying up high,
The balloons blown and reaching the sky.

The tables were set in the red, white and blue,
The dogs were all sniffing at smells that just grew,
For the setting was fine in its red, white and blue
By the sea in the harbour with a wonderful view.

And people all came in their red, white and blue
With pasties and pies and jellies came too
And everyone sat in their red, white and blue.

The games were such fun and Granny came too
Across the sand in her red, white and blue
Turn up the music, we'll sing chorus on cue.

While the light faded and darkness came down
People gradually left, flags dropped on the ground,
Jack's face was still smiling, his day with dear Sue,
Carrying his balloons of red, white and blue.

Sally Crook-Ford

CONNECTION OF FAMILY WITH SLAVERY

Momentous history of slavery emancipation over many passing years
To learn to know
The time of fears and cares
What slavery and its emancipation show

Reflecting on history and historical experiences
No doubting of people also feeling insecure
From the cradle to the grave, a lot of grievances
We see and hear and we can't ignore

Those passing years are bad old days
Where much cruelty prevailed
Much hard work covers the map of slavery
But vision of freedom and all cruelty of the labourers unveiled

The harsh journey into freedom and progress has been slow
Burden untied is for the best
Then comes a time to rejoice as progress grows
After putting slavery in this world to rest.

Lady Olive May McIntosh-Stedman, Laird/Lady of Kincavel

THE SOLDIER

I was only young, just in my teens
Wanted to be in the army, and play with machines.
The day I signed up, my mum was so proud
But I still hear the guns, so heavy and loud.

The boys who signed up, all had smiles on their faces
But we all got to go to some horrible places
Injuries, and wounds and plenty of blood
Sun and damp, the lowlands which flood.

Laughter, smiles, blood, tears and sweat
The loss of some friends, is my only regret
Heroes they will be, forever and a day
And never with machines again will I get to play.

Lisa Fletcher

GLUTTONY

Bess was only ten years old
She lived with Mum and Dad,
She ate enormous dinners
But Mum was very glad.

She thought that eating plenty
Would keep her daughter fit,
And lots of stodgy puddings
Would surely benefit.

But Bess was overeating
Because she loved all food,
Dad noticed that her tummy
Was starting to protrude.

So Mum took Bess to see the doc
Who gave some good advice,
'She's clearly eating far too much
Small portions will suffice.

It must be all the food she eats
She needs to eat more fruit,
These fatty foods and puddings
Really do not suit.'

A regimen was ordered
The doctor made it clear
That Bess must eat more sensibly
But was this too severe?

Poor Bess was hungry all the time
She needed more to eat,
She sobbed and wailed in temper,
So Mum gave her a treat.

A sticky toffee pudding
With custard poured on top,
It tasted so delicious
Bess ate and couldn't stop.

The moral of this story,
Is to make you all aware
That greed may cause some damage,
To your body – so *beware*.

Anne Smith

NOT THE MAN FOR YOU DEAR

When Arabella ffanshawe, with two small 'f's' and an 'e',
Brought a long-haired boy called Wayne home, to meet her parents for tea,
The atmosphere, though quite polite was, shall we say, a trifle tight,
The conversation somewhat trite. They clearly weren't impressed.
And as he rode off down the drive on his battered Honda one-two-five,
Arabella waved goodbye, her parents gave a little sigh and raised their eyes up to the sky.
Then Father took a little walk while wife and daughter had a talk

'My dear, he's not quite what we had in mind; I mean he's really not your kind.
We always imagined the man for you would have a name with a hyphen or two.
Or, failing that, we might just face, a name that began in lower case
And, in a dire emergency, like accidental pregnancy
We'd even take Smythe with an 'e' and a 'y';
But you can't go through life Mrs Smith with an 'i'.
My dear, he's not for you.
And I never realised that Wayne, was actually a proper name.
Your dear papa could never cope with a son-in-law from an Aussie soap.
So tell him that you're through.

At the table he seemed to be rather confused; he'd no idea which knife to use.
And does he ever clean his shoes?
No dear, he's not for you
And furthermore I'm pretty sure that if you saw his family tree –
Well Heaven knows I'm not a snob, but I suspect you'd have a job
To find respectability among the tangled branches there.

Your finishing school in Switzerland, horrendously expensive,
Was meant to prepare you for life at the top.
Now, I've nothing at all against comprehensives,
But I think all this nonsense with Wayne has to stop.
You know what you must do?'

All that was many years ago and I am sure you'd like to know
The outcome of the chat.
Well, Arabella married Wayne, which caused her parents untold pain;
They didn't talk to her again for sometime after that.

They begged her and cajoled her and her father even told her
That he'd cut her from his will without a cent.
But although she thought him mean, Arabella was eighteen
And didn't have to wait for his consent

So on the couple's wedding day, Papa did not give her away;
He took Mama on holiday to somewhere in the sun.
Of course, the marriage wouldn't last; their daughter would discover fast
That life below her station was no fun.

242

Her father placed a little bet that she would soon want to forget
Life in a council maisonette and come back to the fold.
But Wayne was a computer buff, a genius at all that stuff
And very quickly, sure enough, his genius turned to gold.

Computer systems he devised, the industry soon realised,
Would quickly revolutionise the business they were in.
As Wayne astutely shopped around, the multi-nationals clamoured round
And very soon the couple found a new life would begin.

He took the very best advice and found that he could name his price.
He thought ten million would suffice; and kept the copyright.
As money came hand-over-fist, he became a great philanthropist
And, in New Year's Honours list, the monarch dubbed him Knight

Now Mr and Mrs ffanshawe, with two small 'f's' and an 'e',
Can't wait for Arabella to bring Sir Wayne to tea.
And sometimes, just for devilment, the couple will arrive
Dressed in matching leathers on that Honda one-two-five.

And dear old Mrs ffanshawe, still the lady through and through
When asked about her family, the way that people do,
Will smile, pause briefly for effect, and graciously reply,
'My daughter's Lady Smith you know – and they spell it with an 'i'.'

Bryn Strudwick

SHARING AND HOPE

To give is to love, to love is to share,
With people around you everywhere.
No matter how big, no matter how small,
We are God's creatures one and all.

A friendly hello and a smile on your face
Makes the whole world a happier place.
A little time here, a little time there,
No matter how small, it shows that you care.

I close my eyes and I can see,
What life on Earth should really be.
No more tears, no more strife,
Only love and a happy life.

Lasting friendships built on trust,
Loyalty is uppermost.
A helping hand to those in need,
Makes me feel that we'll succeed,
To rebuild a world with no thought of war,
Peace on Earth for evermore.

Valerie M Helliar

MEMORIES OF POP

Sent for more biscuits,
Down the hill in the wind to the shop.
The door on the latch, passed the front room,
The piano and the old sailor's chest,
Passed the steep, treacherously narrow-stepped stairs,
Into the parlour.
The smell of tea in the air,
My grandfather raking the range,
Daisy the dog gobbles a biscuit from his sooty hand.
The calendar always at 1987, his grey hat,
The mandolin in the corner, the old dial telephone,
Memories of my grandfather, memories of Pop.

Paula Elizabeth Redmond

THE CHINK OF LIGHT

You worry
She's gone home to think
She's asked for space
A chance to breathe
It's been five months

Don't panic
My friend
Let her have as long as it takes
At least she meets and greets you
When you go round to visit the kids
That means, the door isn't completely closed

It's far easier to close the door
Than to keep it open
– And, it looks like: she's kept the door
Of communication with you, open.
So, take heart

I'm serious!

Now, just don't go and lose it
Don't behave like the clodhopper you sometimes are

When you encounter her
Don't go on and on like a broken record
Demanding she return home – or anything like that
That's the sure way to turn her off

Step back
Take it easy
Give her space and time
Let her breathe

Don't crowd her
And, one day – *maybe*, not right away
But, one day
You'll win.

Nayyar Shabbir Ahmad

DELICATE LIFETIME

The butterfly lives for three days at most,
Her time is precious and short.
Each moment she captures and holds on to tight,
But there are battles that need to be fought.

Her wings are of confident colours,
She is proud and rightly to be,
Although the most beautiful butterfly,
She has pain that no one can see.

Surviving each day can get tiresome,
But she smiles and continues to fly.
The butterfly knows that after dark clouds,
There is always a warm, sunny sky.

The warmth on her wings gives her freedom,
Her strength is gathered inside.
To work for the life she has built on her own,
With courage, ambition and pride.

Three days is a butterfly's lifetime,
Each second is lived like the last.
She values the present, looks to the future
And learns from her challenging past.

Donna Chadwick

REX INCOGNITO

'He's a dodo!' said his teacher
'And his classwork is a crime.
Never seems to be a minute sitting still
He just can't remember number facts
For any length of time
And his general knowledge totals almost nil.'

'He's a genius!' said his mother
Chatting by her neighbour's wall
'And it makes me proud to know
That he's so bright
From my fourteen of a family
He's the bestest of them all.
Did I tell you? He can even read and write!'

Elizabeth Blacklaw

A MOTHER TO HER DAUGHTER

I used to say
'Think what it's like when it's washed and ironed'
when we were young at 'jumbles'
and your name for me was 'Mumbles'

Our search through all the piles of clothes
would always find a prize
and we'd go home triumphant
with our new but dusty guise

When they were washed and mended
we owned new clothes from old
they seemed to us so special
we had found them I suppose

They were good and bad times
and always shining through
were you
with all your thoughts for me
your friendship warm and true

Life is like those jumble days
and we should both aspire
to nurture it like jumble clothes
handwash and air our fears and woes
smooth creases out with those we love:
remembering those early years
when life was simple, needs were small,
and happiness was village hall
and pleasure spent on jumble days.

Margaret E McComish

YOUR KISS

Intense is the cold in isolation
When the day is dark in clouds
Of sadness sinking through the heart,

Give me the heat of your kiss
And keep me melted,
For without you I would
Surely turn to ice.

Gaye Marie Horne

THIRTY PIECES OF SILVER

For thirty pieces of silver
Judas betrayed his master
Peter, a favourite disciple, denied Jesus thrice,
Declaring and swearing
He never knew the master.

Jesus the meek shepherd of the sheep
Betrayed again by Judas,
With a mocking kiss on the cheek.
The scoffing sign for Roman soldiers
To take hold of Jesus.
Leading Him away to be crucified
On the cross at Calvary.
Judas ran into the temple
Filled with shame and despair
Throwing the thirty pieces of silver
On the temple floor
When he found no one did care
Judas who betrayed the Son of the Living God
Could live with himself no more,
He sealed his awful doom
Going out the temple door
Thirty pieces of silver lay scattered
On the temple floor.
Judas went out and hanged himself
His guilt he could stand no more,
Jesus was denied, betrayed, crucified,
The price He paid His blood was shed,
At a place called Calvary.
We are bought at a price.
The price of Jesus' precious blood.

Frances Gibson

COCKERMOUTH, THE PRIDE OF CUMBRIA

This is the place I call my town
Surrounded by places I love to roam
Here you can see the places to go
Lovely fells and valleys below.

The lakes are within a few miles away
Lovely Bassenthwaite Lake surrounded
By hill, flowers and trees
Just a few minutes and you are there.

This is the town in which we live
Just look around, there is so much to give
People move up from the south
Must pass the word from mouth to mouth.

As time goes by there is so much to say
See it all, there is not much to pay
The buses travel all around the lakes
So enjoy it all for what it takes.

William Banks

LIFE IS FRAGILE

In our despair
We call unto God
Who hears our prayers
His healing love
Wraps so tight
From dullness
Shines so bright
His ways
Are not our ways
His grace
Living through each day.

Maureen Thornton

CHOICES

Choices – we make them all our life –
Shall I be naughty?
Shall I be good?
Could try both and see what it brings!
What shall I do at school?
Who will decide my course for me?
Parents, teachers or myself?
Should I go to university,
Or travel round the world?
Maybe I'll try both and live life to the full,
What of my lifestyle?
Maybe I will have children
Will I feel repressed or free to choose?
When I grow old what then,
Where will I live?
Who will make the choice, myself, health or family?
Life from its very beginning to its end is
Choice – choice – choice
Until the day God calls us home
That day we do not choose.

Shirley Ludlow

STRESS

We spend our time harassing
It's easier than gassing
We hoot, we stare, we shout, we care!
At your back we are there
Get some peace, if you dare,
Our scribblings are noted
For being misquoted
And causing warfare
We will be judged for sending you,
To an early grave
But we don't care
Spying pays our super bills.

Irene Grant

250

SHOPPING IN HAMPSTEAD

As I walked home from the village today
I heard a bird begin to sing
I looked up to the top of the tree
To try to see what bird it might be
For it was such a heavenly sound
That drifted back to me on the ground

On the Heath there are children at play
Nannies push them on the swings
The lilac trees are in full bloom
The willows wave in unison
All are heralds of the return of spring

I stop to feed the ducks and geese
They gobble and fight to get a piece
I sit on the green
How lucky I am,
That I'm not stuck in a traffic jam.

Pamela Baily

UNIQUE

You are unique
Just be yourself
Stand proud and tall
With inner strength
Love all your ways
Be true to you
Praise all the little
Things you do
Have nothing to prove
Just know your worth
A treasure put down
Upon this Earth
Hug yourself
So special you
Unique in everything you do.

Kathleen June Jinks

GRAFFITI

Have faith
It's all disclosed
On Flanagan's wall,
Set out and staged
For the twenty-first century.
The writing writ large
On Jungian dreams
And Liverpool tables.

The meaning is in the making of meaning.
Underground wandering
In honeycomb lairs
Inscribed with '23 Skidoo'
On gold manhole covers
Covering a multitude of sins
In vinyl silk and women's underwear.

We are in a cage of zoo.
Left in a cold morning breeze
Down the Mathew Street highway
Escaped to perfection
By holy roller coasters
Signposting the 'end of the world'
To secret pilgrims.
The only words left
Graffiti'd on Eric's board
'We are all in a state of fluxus now'.
'The situation and context is everything'.
As the last tramp
Closes the large double-edged door
And takes a ferry trip on the Mersey, home.

Peter Corbett

BLACK SNOW, LIVERPOOL 1937

We stand on the corner, hands in pockets
And shoulders hunched

Nothing to do and nowhere to go, a dispirited
And motley bunch

No job, no money, no aims in life,
Nothing to give the kids or the wife

Pockets are empty and life is bare,
No stories to tell just stand and stare

The sky is grey and it looks like snow,
The city is cold and faces are white

A good heavy fall will bring work tonight

An army of men with shovel and brush
Will clear the streets for tomorrow's rush

Grey-clad figures poorly dressed,
A cap, old trousers, a jacket and vest

An old scarf crossed and tucked in tight
To fight the cold and this long dark night

Some men will drop before this night is through
So weak and hungry, they always do

The snow must be cleared for the traffic to flow
And the poor old horses with heavy carts in tow

Tram wheels only grip on snow-free tracks,
To get them cleared will break our backs

We work through the night cold and wet
For the chance to earn money we rarely get

The snow in the country is fluffy and white,
Very different to what we see here tonight

The flakes are white as they float down,
But turn to black slush when they hit the ground

The snow must be deep for the top to stay white,
Oh God it's cold, this never-ending night

We're here tonight to earn some dough,
So we might as well move some more black snow.

Maurice Shea

NATURE'S MAGNIFICENCE

The last two golden streaks have left the sky
Not masked by twilight's darkening fall,
But by black, ominous, threatening clouds
Rolling in from land to cover all
The town, the sand, the sea and clifftops bare

The clouds they come at first with gentle roar
As lightning lights the scene with bright display.
Flash lightning, fearsome but spectacular,
Outshining any firework display.
A moment's lull as thick the black clouds come.

As eerie silence falls; the street lights fail.
The thunder roars and louder, louder grows,
Until fork lightning splits the darkling scene;
A mighty crash that shocks the world anew
And sends the raindrops hurtling to the Earth.

Towards the cliffs the screeching seagull soars,
While rabbit, mouse and fox search out their lairs,
The parched earth greedily soaks up the rain,
As flowers bow their heads in fervent prayer
For now they know that they will live again.

The fury of the storm is spent at last
Clouds roll across the melancholy sea.
Late sun shines down in golden victory
And flowers raise their heads and smile in glee,
Majestic nature – oh so little Man.

Barbara Dunning

GHOST LADY OF LANGHOLM

Ghost lady of Langholm, by chance we should meet,
As I awaited the flute band in the High Street.
You appeared, like an angel in the mist and the rain
Another glance, you're gone, will I see you again?

The following day, when rain turned to shine,
Your appearance again, by the footbridge so fine.
Your smile filled the air with the sweet smell of flowers
That moment, I knew, I'd remember for hours.

The band will play a sweet melody,
And the beat of the drums brings you closer to me.
With hair so fine almost shining like gold
No one would believe a story so bold.

Oh lady, you came out of nowhere and you stand there so tall,
Against the stonework of the cemetery wall.
With a long dress that seems forever flowing
And dark eyes so bright and glowing
It is a meeting that lives with me yet
On that misty morning, both soaking wet.

As you emerge in valley, the sunlight will explode
From the dark treetops and onto the road.
In the distance you will fade into the haze
Oh lady, you'll always amaze.

Over the heather and across a wee burn
Ghost lady will you ever return,
You're just a memory now, was it my imagination or perhaps a dream?
You never came back, so I never knew
Did this really happen or was it too much of the Malt Barley Brew?

Brian Ritchie

STILL LIFE WITH BIRD

The yellowing blacks of green dispel
Clouds that cross a plaintive sky
None of the dazzle yet can quell
The raging this July.

Out of the gloom stretches a starling
In silhouette an albatross
Poised for flight yet faltering
As on the cliffs at Galapagos.

Here a boy fair as Hylas
Grew to manhood over the years
Can anyone dare rest in this place?
Only through tears.

The yellowing blacks of green enshroud
The dazzle beneath this plaintive sky
Though sun climbs to sizzle through cloud
Still blistering borders cry.

Rosemary Benzing

BETRAYAL

Passion spent with the
Wrong name still
Scalding my lips and
Shed tears' salt dry
On my cheeks.
Strangers now, accusing
Fingers of pain shielding
The sunlight from the
Crack in the wall above
The pillow where I had lain.
Below the window the
Grasses shudder and sigh
Impossible shadows cross
The pattern etched in the
Sweat folds of my hands.
A garment clings to the quilt,
Crumpled to size and
Still warm to the touch.
Just leave now, from the
Well of the stairs, the
Windows are closed
And the shutters are down.

Marion Gunther

RAIN AND SNOW

Train hesitates;
we're all worried about being late.

Train tarries too long; where did we go wrong?
Should have got a car or caught a plane.

But

we could be on another train;
looking out at driving rain
or drifts of snow wondering, where is it we go?
wondering where it is we go?

With anxious children's eyes:
we have to tell them dreadful lies;
as through the bleakest land we go,
through driving rain,
or drifts of snow.

Instead of angry that our train is late;
we could be
almost conscious of our fate.

Huddled up close, in threadbare clothes,
divested of all history, of what makes us
you and me; shoved into the uncomprehending
crowd; *and rain and snow*
will be our shroud.

It is my anxious fervent prayer,
that those haunted trains did not get there;
that all those pitiful men and women were escorted
straight to Heaven.

And all the children especially
blessed; so all the guards received were *husks.*

And do you know and strange to tell,
that butterflies survive in hell?

Next time you're livid that your train is late
think of those people and their fate.

And all those souls who have no choice
and are denied their human voice;
and try not to retaliate and fill their days with
rage and hate.

Like the threadbare people on those trains
looking out at driving rain, wondering where it is

they go;

their only shroud the rain and snow.

Rain and snow,

Rain

and snow,

Rain

and snow

Rain and snow

Rain and

snow.

Ingrid Andrew

WAR

War is a demon, that haunts the mind of man,
Causing misery and destruction in life's eternal plan.
Our triumphs and our conquests, our laughter and our joy
Can all so quickly vanish in the blink of an eye.

The planes and the rockets, the tanks and the guns
Are all Man's creation to bring destruction in our time.
What games are we playing with life, death and trust,
Another futile test of strength, so we can pin medals on our chest.

Perhaps we're still like children who like to play with toys,
Then to fight one another, just to see who'll win first prize.
Our generals and our heads of state just shake their heads and bow
But it's our men who go off to war and gamble with their lives.

We've fought from the dawn of time, must we fight until its end
Or look at one another, not as enemies, but as friends.
Life is too precious to be lost in some damned war,
Better to live our lives in peace and love, than to fight for evermore.

Gwyn Thomas

STEVE

(This poem is dedicated to my late brother-in-law, Stephen Finn, who passed away on 17 May 2012)

I can't remember where
I first met my husband's big brother
But I do remember, Steve
Once I cooked breakfast for you,
In your mum's kitchen in Athlone
You polished off the sausages
But you did not eat your toast.

I can't remember how often
We visited or met
But I do remember, Steve
What you looked like on your wedding day
Like the cat that got the cream and more
That morning you couldn't wait
To get to your bride

I can't remember how many times
I saw you in the High Street
But I do remember, Steve
How you always greeted me
With a hand kiss, full of Irish charm
And usually in the company of your wife

Blue eyes with a naughty twinkle
Under bushy eyebrows
Sideburns
Elvis fan
Rough around the edges
But a gentleman at heart
That's how I will remember you Steve
We loved you, just as you were.

Martine Finn

GD

Teddy-boy suit,
Winklepicker shoes,
'Tommy Steel' singin' the blues
He's top of the league
A real 'Wayne Rooney'
Likes a bit of 'This ol' House'
Loves Rosemary Clooney –
He told me that he once
Played in a band
'The Beatles?' I asked.
'Nay, lad, Jimmy Shand.'
Always up front,
And straight to the point,
'The Land of the Few'
I've heard tell, he's next in line,
To play the 'new' Doctor Who –

Like 'Arkright' he's open all hours –
He'll sit and chat, about this and that,
And probably tell you about the time
He appeared on 'Jackanory'
Failing that, he'll more than likely
Give you his own rendition of
'Land of Hope and Glory'.
On that note, 'Dear Reader,'
Here endeth my story.

Ted Brookes

WELCOME TO MY WORD COLLECTION

Some folks collect gilt-edged antiques
But I'm a word collecting freak;
They're found in each and every book
And on signs and billboards if you look

I collect the lyrics of thousands of songs
And make notes whenever I'm out among
The chatterers in my corner shop
And at my bus stop; I collect the lot.

I love see-sawing words that rhyme
Like freedom after doing time,
I love words fuzzy, warm and witty,
Not pompous, haughty, cold or prickly;

Please lace them with your heart's affection
And not cerebral-cold dissection.
I've made-up words such as 'Pizzazz!'
Like musical language; verbal jazz.

I've nonsense words made up for fun
Which work when sense has been outdone.
When asked my favourites by a chatshow host,
I'd no doubt, 'Your cheque's in the post!'

Some words can mean just what they say
But others lie to earn their pay;
We make some up so we can lie;
'Though sticks and stones . . .' some make me cry.

My cat can't tell me what she wants
Though I'm quite clear of my response
So she will not face libel suits
But words offend and can confuse

Like Chinese whispers which occurred
When General's spoken order blurred
From, 'Send more troops and we'll advance!'
To, 'Send me four pence for our dance!'

Some words are worth a thousand pounds,
While others are buried in landfill ground;
The most valued in my collection
Is secret in police protection . . .

The rest are here to share with you
Please help yourself to one or two . . .
They're almost free and guaranteed
That, since we're all collectors too,
My collection's 'specially for you.

William Greig

PARTY TIME

We thought we'd have a party, it was such a lovely spread.
My mum was working through the night, but I went up to bed.
I don't know when I crawled upstairs, I know it was quite late,
My mum has so much energy, I couldn't stand the pace.

I awoke this morning and made a cup of tea, there she was my dear old mum asleep on the settee.
Many friends were coming, some from far away, if the night turned foggy, we'd tell them they could stay.

We thought we'd covered everything then remembered; 'No balloons!'
We still had time to get some before the afternoon.
Our dog would keep her eye on things until we both got back
We left in such a hurry and forgot about the cat.

I'd covered all the food up as best I was able,
Clingfilm's not such easy stuff to spread across the table.
When we got back and feeling tired we both had to agree,
One thing would revive us, we'd make a cup of tea.

I never thought, nor did expect the sight that would confront us,
Trifles flying through the air, oh! What a blooming rumpus.
Chicken legs were flying followed closely by the cat,
My dish of best red salmon gone, so that was the end of that!

I'd taken so much trouble to make that chocolate log,
Not much left of that I saw, enjoyed by the dog!
We couldn't disappoint our friends but what else could we do?
'I think I'd better ring them, and say we've caught the flu.'

Jean Windle

BIG SIS KATH

Sadly it's time to say goodbye to my beloved big sister Kath,
I never expected this yet,
It's shocked us all and happened much too fast.
I've not had the chance to tell you all the things I should,
Like thanks for always being there for me, I only wish I could,
Get one last big hug from you and tell you how much I love you,
I'm so glad you were my big sister,
I'm gonna miss you greatly too.
I wish I could be more like you,
Seize chances and not let life pass me by,
I only know that from now on
I'm certainly going to try!
I've always admired your confidence
Strength and the fact you lived life to the full,
You had so many knocks and setbacks along the way,
But life with you was certainly never dull!
Nothing seemed to faze you,
You just faced up to whatever life threw at you,
Be it a new partner, house, family, job
You even found time for lots of hobbies too.
Always so smartly dressed, usually in your high stilettos
Always full of fun and you always loved a dance,
Ready for any new challenge, bring it on,
You were never scared to take a chance.
I've always envied your looks, personality
And I'm very proud to have had you as my beloved big sis
I'm gonna miss you so very, very much Kath
And that's why I'm now writing this.
Because I never got the chance to tell you all this,
I should have made more time for you,
But I thought we'd years ahead of us,
To share more precious moments and new experiences too
You've been around in my life and there for me,
Since the day in 1951, when I was born
Now suddenly and oh so sadly
All trace of you is gone
I just hope you didn't suffer much
And you died knowing little pain,
But you've left behind so many people
Who would have loved to have you back here again.

So night, night, God bless, dearest sister,
Looking back on a life filled with so much joy and pain,
Here's hoping I can follow in your footsteps,
Party hard and long, until hopefully one day we meet up again.
Your little sis Dot.

Dorothy Ridings

THE AFTERMATH

After the storm
Windowpanes steam
In the autumn sunshine.
Uprooted trees lie
Spread-eagled on the ground,
Their blood-red leaves
Strewn across the road –
A casualty of nature's battlefield.

After the battle
Guns fall silent
For a brief interlude.
Time to tend to wounded
And collect the dead,
Their life blood spent,
Turning the earth red –
A casualty of man's battlefield.

Patricia McKenna

THE HARMONY OF RHYME

Should you aspire towards a celestial choir
The harmony of rhyme will always inspire.
A melody is found in poetry
A sentence flows and all words compose,
Into tuneful verse and melodious prose.
A mood is met and the meter set
With phonetic tones from the alphabet.
An orchestral score extraordinary;
A rhapsody of rhyme and of harmony.
With symphonies of syllables set in a time sublime
There is set a medley there with a lilting air,
An arrangement of prose with a rhyming flair.
Theme phrases intrude suiting the mood
Serenading each tuneful fugue.
There are harmonious sounds in the poetic company
Of celestial senses inspired by harmony
Should you aspire towards a celestial choir
The harmony of rhyme will always inspire.

Stan Coombs

SCAR FACE

I have a scar upon my face,
I wish it would disappear,
Nobody is friends with me and
No one wants me near.

I'm as ugly as a monster,
I'm frightened like a mouse,
I'm terrified of going out,
I stay within my house.

I wish that it would go away,
And let me live my life,
I wish I could have happiness,
And end this tortured life.

If only life was easier,
Or I could have a friend so true,
It wouldn't really matter then
To be the real you.

Stella Lynne Longwell

SOUL

Soul came in the dead of night
Attracted by the light
Tapping at the window,
Calling out loud and clear,
Should I venture our and overcome my fear?
Soul came in the dead of night,
Attracted by the light
Opening the door and looking
Down the drive, through a
Misty unclear light.
Soul came in the dead of night,
Attracted by the light.
I started to question in an aggressive tone,
But as it moved and walked away,
I was later to find the seed was sown,
The deed was done.
Soul came in the dead of night,
Attracted by the light.
Some time later, don't know how long
We were to touch,
It was so strong.
Soul came in the dead of night,
Attracted by the light.
Will my soul return?
How long must I wait until it returns,
What's mine?
Soul came in the dead of night,
Attracted by the light.

Rod Pilkington

ENDGAME

Sharp-edged
The fields of youth,
Stained with blood
Of badger,
Black on white,
White on black,
Chess endgame . . .
Don't blame me.
I've never seen a badger,
Anyway

And otter,
Slip-sliding;
Synchronised
Swimmer extraordinaire,
Lithe,
Mortal mammal . . .
Well, I have to confess,
I've never seen an otter,
Either.

Look,
No need to be concerned,
They're enmeshed in
National Geographic,
Netted on the Internet;
Click and press view graphics,
Glorious, neat synopsis
Of habit and habitat.
There's even sound and movement
With an up-to-date app.

Blackbird's song?
I can pipe it
Into the garden
Straight from my PC,
Download images
From my digital camera.
I don't need to bother
With fur and feather.
I haven't got time
For all that conservation stuff,
Anyway.

Sandy Davies

THE BUDGIES

Last Christmas for Becky for a treat
I bought a budgie that went *tweet, tweet*
We loved that little bird you know
We'd watch it fly to and fro
And then it would get on its little swing
And ring its little bell, *ding-a-ling-ling*
I said to Becky, 'I think you will find
It needs a little mate that bird of thine.'
We got him a mate of the very best
I said to the man, 'Ger rid of the rest,'
Well you could see they were in love from the start
We had a job to keep them apart
We'd open the cage to let them out for a fly
There they'd go, my oh my
One day I came home and opened the door
There were feathers all over the floor
I said, 'Oh my God, who could do this to me?
Those cats have eaten my birdie for tea.'
I rang up my sister, 'Now don't you get stressed
You will find this is life I guess
Come up the club and have a drink
It will stop you stressing I would think'
I went up the club and said, 'I'm in mourning'
They all looked at me and started yawning
You could see they didn't care about my loss
In fact they couldn't give a toss
Then someone put a card on the stage
Saying: *For sale nice new cage*
I said, 'The window was open wide
Do you think they might have flown outside?'
'They wouldn't have any feathers would they now
So they wouldn't be able to fly very well.'
'Oh what a hoot, unless they had a parachute.'
These are the friends that I have got
Although again I will say not
So next time I am feeling stressed
I will go to a stranger, I think that will be best!

Pat Newbury

WORDS

Words

There are such a great amount
But how many really count?
Some talk drivel all day
And yet have nothing to say.

Words

They grace countless pages
Of books lasting through the ages,
Sometimes deceitful like Iago liars
Or as angry as forest fires.

Words

They can be beautiful as well
But I have a sorry story to tell
For the words just spoken by you
Have broken my poor heart in two.

Guy Fletcher

THAT'S ONE CLASSY CAT

A classy sort of gal, so she seemed to me,
Strolling down the avenue, a look of captivating glee,
She will eat you up and take all that you are,
Then on her way to another, what a star!

No preening or fussy overtures to enhance the mood,
Nor will she take, any amount of exotic food,
No tempting the temptress, for she alone is the flirt,
Ignore if you can but she will only treat you as dirt.

When the fun is over, away to pastures new,
She wants no one, nor does she want you,
She plays and turns heads to seek a thrill,
Then bury you with contempt with a girlish will!

Now she's old the days have passed by,
As she lives out her life on cushions lie,
No more siren, just old and tired,
Lost all the class and the once energy fired.

Sheila Ellen Wright

UNDERSTANDING THE FEELINGS OF HOMOSEXUALS

The hurt that we feel inside,
is due to the years we had to hide.
When the damage is done,
we have nowhere else to run.
For society to look down on us,
for them not to treat them like dust.
As for years we have been scared,
as we walk while people stared.
As the same-sex will walk,
while we hear whispers and talk.
While the inside is sore,
hoping you have the key to open the door.
As we live and hope,
as we are finding it hard to cope.
As the next generation will not feel as bad,
for as the older generation will be so glad.
Hoping for love to be there,
but its getting hard to bear.
As we are gay,
we will have our say.
We will not be looked down upon,
and people thinking it's wrong.
We cannot change how we are,
we will not run and get in our car.
As two men shall lay,
as they lay night and day.
As we are proud,
we will fight and be very loud.
As love is love,
while the two men lay like turtle doves.
For the pain to go,
knowing it will take some time and be very slow.
As to all my people, please be strong,
as we know it's not wrong.

Neil Douglas Tucker

UNTITLED

Beauty laid on bloom of youth.
Shone through his unburdened manner.
He looked through the window
At a greater galaxy than I.
A fleeting realisation,
An undefined awareness
Cast a veil across that calm countenance.

Distant planets felt his silent plea.
Felt his accusations trembling through space.
Wound the powerful shockwaves
Around Saturn, as cloth of gold,
Coiling them to breaking point
To reinforce intergalactic harmony,
Reserving dialogue for future analysis
For considerations, and conclusions.

Heard sounds of centuries babbling disorientated music,
Crashing through Earth's exosphere,
Driving forth, like countless crab nebulas
Exploding upon eternity,
Seeking God, in any form.

Then I walked on past the window.

Irene Leah Hazell

REMINISCENCE

When I was young things weren't like now
We had to struggle on somehow
Food was rationed, so were clothes
How people managed, goodness knows
Our folk worked hard to make ends meet
To pay for shoes upon our feet
And our large family had to be fed
Three or four slept in one bed
The only toilet was on the stair
Three other families had to share
No electric, gas was the light
Made eerie shadows in the night
Accumulators for radios
No TV, laptops or things like those
A horse and cart delivered coal
The coalman carried it, poor soul
To the school we had to walk
No jotters, just a slate and chalk
No uniforms, they were too dear
We had to wear our usual gear
On the way home we'd race a tram
And hurry home to our dear mam.

Margaret Rankin

MY DAUGHTER'S THOUGHTS (ABOUT HER STROKE)

I'm floating on a sea of red
Am I alive or am I dead?
Some people talking very loud
There seems to be an awful crowd.

I drift away to a land of dreams
But not for long or so it seems,
For they are calling out my name,
For weeks they call it just the same.

My head is hot, I've got a pain,
And all they do is call out, 'Jane!'
A cool hand rests upon my head
I must be here, I can't be dead!

They pull me up, they put me down
They turn me over, pull me around.
They've pricked and punctured every bit,
Now there's a wheelchair for me to sit.

I'll try my voice, now that tube's out
Why do I whisper when I want to shout?
Why should I bother? Why should I care?
I'll give them the blank look, the vacant stare.

My mother's tough, she's tough with me,
She sees things the others don't see.
She nags and nags and sings a lot,
She wants me to use the voice I've got.

The physios are really good,
They push me hard the way they should.
But where are the nurses who tried and tried
And carried on till I replied?

It's quiet in here and boy it's hot.
I know Heaven is cool and Hell is not!
I don't want to stay here anymore,
I want to know what they have in store.

Judy Hopkin

AN UNEVENTFUL JOURNEY

As I gaze out my window in the morning,

I see a vision of a freshly incarnation of supposingly crystal-clear daylight.

An eventful outbreak adds a spark of sensation to a terrible tailored day.

Believe it or not, a life without events depicts a body without a soul.

Problems reassures ones continuity to live a catastrophic life.

No problems given no reasoning to push forward in search of discovering forthcoming answers.

To find a success sensational, one must have suffered, to fully appreciate its eloquence.

Amir Motlagh

FORWARD POETRY INFORMATION

We hope you have enjoyed reading this book - and that you will continue to enjoy it in the coming years.

If you like reading and writing poetry drop us a line, or give us a call, and we'll send you a free information pack.

Alternatively if you would like to order further copies of this book or any of our other titles, then please give us a call or log onto our website at www.forwardpoetry.co.uk.

Forward Poetry Information
Remus House
Coltsfoot Drive
Peterborough
PE2 9BF
(01733) 890099